Local Self-G

Blerim Burjani

Local Self-Governance
Reform in Kosovo

Dictus Publishing

Publisher:
Dictus Publishing
is a trademark of
Dodo Books Indian Ocean Ltd. and OmniScriptum S.R.L publishing group

120 High Road, East Finchley, London, N2 9ED, United Kingdom
Str. Armeneasca 28/1, office 1, Chisinau MD-2012, Republic of Moldova, Europe

ISBN: 978-613-7-35696-8

Instituti i Kosovës për Politika Zhvillimore (IKPZH)

BLERIM BURJANI

Local Self-Governance Reform in Kosovo

PRISTINA ,2018

BLERIM BURJANI

Local Self-Governance Reform in Kosovo

3

Content :

4

5

INTRUDUCTION

Kosovo local institutions was establish since 2000, until that time was a many debate in political and international level according to establish process of decentralizations, Kosovo now is country decentralized, and now is period trying to think about local government reform step by step, it was during of this road many interesting developments according to this level of function local democracy. Some international councils, NGO have being active starting from UNMIK and the Council of Europe who have proposed how to consolidate local government and to make operative and desirable for accomplish interest of citizens of different nationalities in Kosovo. The local elections was organized for the first time in Kosovo in 2000, and those at the national level in 2001. The organization of the first local elections was aimed at starting the functioning of local government.

After the war, the Provisional Government of Kosovo had appointed the mayors of the municipals, then current municipalities up to the organization of local elections so that there would be no stagnation in governance at the local level and that the citizens would have representatives in the local government until the new election mention up . The Interim Administrative Council of UNMIK and the Transitional Council with several committees to supplement the institutional acting until the made election in local level. Political parties in Kosovo, UNMIK, OSCE were interested in organizing local elections as soon as possible and building a well-functioning, democratic and multi-ethnic local government. Since 2000, several debates have been organized and various political representatives and personalities from civil society have been invited to find a form of regulation for the functioning of local government.

UNMIK had therefore issued Regulations 2000/45[1] and 2000/49[2] in this area, which was slightly incompatible and contradictory in terms of contradictions referring to local government in Kosovo. Since 2000, it has been intended for local government reform, and later the international community decided that Kosovo should take decentralization, and for that purpose the Council of Europe is starting to deal with decentralization in Kosovo.

---

[1] UNMIK, Regulations 2000/45[1] and 2000/49
[2] UNMIK,Regulations 2000/45[2] and 2000/49

6

There were also many meetings at the political and expert level to find reasonable grounds for switching to decentralization, as Kosovo's Constitutional Framework did not foresee decentralization, but made a political decision to have decentralization in Kosovo. The PISG at that time had reservations about the concept of ethnic decentralization later "silently" and with Vienna's negotiations about Kosovo's status was accepted the ethnic concept of decentralization that had reactions by intellectuals and experts, but all that happened was decentralization quite specific that laid the foundations of Vienna at political level. And Law for Self-Governance was approved by Parliament of Republic of Kosovo in 20 February 2008[3].

MLGA continued its work in organizing administrative work and had worked towards its priorities. It was important for the MLGA to deal with the established annual priorities; the Kosovo Parliament has issued the Law on Local Self-Government. Kosovo has announced independence on February 17, 2008. Local government development in Kosovo has been followed by several stages, post-war period, local elections organized in Kosovo in 2000, which is the beginning of the establishment of local government, the second stage of decentralization, the third stage of consolidation, and is expected to start reforming the power local and needs to be reviewed also the law on local self-government. It is necessary to review the large number of municipalities that are more municipalities extracted from politics but not necessarily in some small municipalities of Kosovo cannot be carried out some basic services, so these municipalities should be revised if they need to remain a municipality or join a nearby commune. The local government with several municipalities like Pristina has been modernized in providing services to the citizens, while still is necessary working with some other municipalities to improve these services.

Local Institutions

Local self-government It is more and more useful economically, politically and sociologically since law is just a tool[4]. The municipality is a territorial political community of a state or a unit of its own. Local institutions are committed to the functioning of the economic and social, educational and health life of citizens, civil society organizations, political parties, local media, which can influence the overall

[3] Law for Self-Governance was approved by Parliament of Republic of Kosovo in 20 February 2008.
[4] Decentralization and Local Governance in South Eastern Europe and Southern Caucasus,pp13, 2011

life with the influential capacities in the management of the fields determined by legal and constitutional competencies .Efficiency of its administrative work, and the democratic accountability of local government.

CHAPTER ONE

1. Legal definition for municipality

This law defines the legal status of municipalities, their competencies and general principles of municipal finances, organization and functioning of the municipal bodies, the intra-municipal arrangements and the inter-municipal cooperation including the cross border cooperation and the relationship between municipalities and central government. The City of Pristina, as the capital city of Republic of Kosovo, shall be regulated by a separate Law on the City of Pristina. The Law on Local Self-Government shall apply to the City of Pristina except as may be provided for otherwise in the Law on the City of Pristina. Separate legislation may be adopted to grant a special status and competencies to other cities. Allowing terms shall have the meaning indicated below, unless the context within which such term appears clearly intends another meaning: -"Charter,"- shall mean the European Charter of Local Self-Government, as adopted by the Council of Europe on the 15th of October 1985. -"Community,"- shall mean a group of communities belonging to the same ethnic, religious, or linguistic group. -"Government,"- means the Government of Republic of Kosovo; -"Citizen"- shall have the meaning ascribed to it in [Article 10 of the present Law on Statehood]. -"Local Self-government"- shall mean the right and ability of local authorities as established by this law and within the limits thereof, to regulate and manage a substantial share of public affairs under their own responsibility and in the interest of the local population; -"Municipality,"- shall mean the basic unit of local self-government in Republic of Kosovo, made up of citizens of communities of a specified territory defined by law as stipulated to in the Law on the Number, Names and Municipal Boundaries 2007.

Municipal Assembly is the highest representative body of the municipality consisting of all its elected members and Mayo-is the highest executive body of the municipality elected through direct elections. Principle of Subsidiary means that the public affairs shall be dealt with as closely as possible to the citizens of the municipality by the lowest level of government that is able to provide public services efficiently for citizen. According to law own competencies shall mean competencies vested upon the municipalities by the Constitution or laws for which they are fully responsible in insofar as they concern the local interest and in accordance with the law; Delegated Competencies from Center to local institutions shall mean competencies of the central government and other central institutions the execution of which is temporarily assigned by law to municipalities. -"Enhanced competencies" by law shall mean competencies vested upon a municipality or a number of municipalities by law. "Administrative Review" is the right and ability of central government institutions to review the legality of the activity of the local authorities in the area of own and enhanced competencies and the legality and expediency of their activity in the area of delegated competencies. Supervisory authority according to law, shall mean the ministry responsible for the local government and/or other institutions of the Government of Republic of Kosovo in their respective areas of responsibility. "Review of legality"- shall mean the review conducted by the supervisory authority to ensure that municipal acts have been issued in conformity with applicable legal provisions and that the issuing body has not acted in excess of its legally recognized mandate. "Review of expediency" shall mean the review conducted by the supervisory authority to ensure that delegated competencies have been executed in compliance with the rules, criteria and standards determined by the central government and if the measures taken by municipality were appropriate to achieve the results determined by the Government of Republic of Kosovo. -"Majority vote"- shall mean a vote that requires the assent of more than one half of the members present and voting at the meeting at which the proposal is considered. This is the default mechanism by which decisions of Municipal Assembly shall be brought. - "Two thirds (2/3) majority"- shall mean a vote that requires the assent of 2/3 of all the members of the Municipal Assembly, Ministry", shall mean the ministry responsible for local government unless the context clearly refers otherwise; - "Statute of the Municipality, shall mean the highest act adopted by the Municipal Assembly in accordance with the Constitutions and the laws regulating the internal organization of the municipality. "Rule of Procedure"- shall mean an act adopted by the Municipal Assembly providing the rules of order and conduct: "Municipal regulation"- shall mean an act adopted by the required number of the Municipal Assembly regulating a certain area of the municipal competencies.

2. MUNICIPALITY

Municipality is the basic unit of local self-government in Republic of Kosovo, made up of community of citizens of a specific territory defined by law and shall exercise all powers which are not explicitly reserved for the central institutions, to develop local democracy and local economic infrastructure, primary and secondary education, social and family medicine, local transport and to perform other competencies reserved by law for local governance. All municipal organs shall ensure that the citizens of the municipality enjoy all rights and freedoms without distinction of any kind, such as race, ethnicity, color, sex, language, religion, political or other opinion, national or social origin, property, birth, or other status, and that they have fair and equal opportunities in municipality service at all levels. Municipalities shall implement their policies and practices to promote coexistence and peace between their citizens and to create appropriate conditions enabling all communities to express, preserve, and develop their national, ethnic, cultural, religious, and linguistic identities. All municipal authorities shall be answerable to the citizens of the Municipality in the forms set by law. Citizens of the municipality shall have the right to participate in the activities of the municipality, as prescribed by law. Municipalities shall be entitled to enter into agreements with villages, quarter or settlements within their territory to offer services closer to citizens in accordance with Article 35[5] and their statutes. Legal Status of the Municipality shall be legal person. As a legal person, each municipality shall have the legal capacity to, inter alia: a) sue and be sued in the courts; b) own and manage property; c) be owner or co-owner of any company that is of interest to municipality in relation to citizens; d) enter into contracts; e) engage staff; and f) engage in other activities that are necessary for discharging its responsibilities. Names and Boundaries Municipalities shall have their names and boundaries as described in the Law on Administrative Boundaries of Municipalities and may only be changed in accordance with that law.[6]

3. Symbols and policy

Municipalities shall have their own symbols including the coats of arms, seals, emblems, and municipal flags. Municipalities shall use a seal that includes the sign and name of the Municipality. The symbols of a Municipality shall be approved and changed by the municipal assembly pursuant to the constitutional and legal provisions of Republic of Kosovo and shall not resemble to symbols of other states or municipalities within or outside Republic of Kosovo. The symbols of a

---

[5] Law for Local Self-Governance of Republic of Kosovo , Article 35
[6] Law for Local Self-Governance of Republic of Kosovo

municipality may be approved or changed by two thirds (2/3) majority vote of the Municipal Assembly after extensive public consultation has taken place.[7]

Citizens of Republic of Kosovo A citizen of the Municipality is any person who is a habitual citizen of Republic of Kosovo, living in the respective Municipality.

4. Languages

The use of languages in the Municipality shall be regulated in accordance with the applicable law on the use of languages. The Municipal Assembly has adopt detailed municipal regulations on the use of languages within its territory as set out in the applicable law on the use of languages in Kosovo.

5. Municipal Bodies

The organs of a municipality are the Municipal Assembly and the Mayor. Acts of the Municipal Organs Municipal Assembly and Mayor have the right to enact acts and take any implementation measure within their areas of competence. All municipal acts shall comply with the constitutional and legal system of Republic of Kosovo.

6. Acts of the Municipal Assembly

The Municipal Assembly may adopt acts within their areas of its competences according to free will of legal representative of citizens. Acts of the Municipal Assembly shall be effective in force in the all territory of the Municipality enacting the act. These acts s include:[8] a) Statute of the Municipality; b) Rules of Procedure; c) Municipal regulations; and d) any other acts necessary or proper for efficient operation of the Municipality. The Statute of the Municipality shall be adopted and may be amended by at least a two thirds vote of the Municipal Assembly.. The Rules of Procedure shall be adopted and may be amended, when necessary, by a majority vote of the Municipal Assembly.[9]

7. Acts of the Municipal Mayor

The Municipal Mayor shall have the right to issue instructions and decisions within his areas of competence.

---

[7] Law for Local Self-Governance of Republic of Kosovo
[8] Law for Local Self-Governance of Republic of Kosovo , Article 12
[9] Law for Local Self-Governance of Republic of Kosovo

8. Property of the Municipality

Municipalities have the right to own and manage immovable and movable properties. Municipalities have the right as well to sell and lease the immovable and movable property according to law enforce , with the exception of the sale of the land that will be regulated by a special law. Municipalities shall keep and maintain the Register of all movable and immovable property owned or occupied by the municipality.

9. Principle of Subsidiary

The municipalities exercise its competences in accordance with the principle of subsidiary. Municipal Competencies Municipalities exercise own, delegated and enhanced competencies in accordance with the law.

10. Own Competencies

Municipalities have full and exclusive powers, insofar as they concern the local interest, while respecting the standards set forth in the applicable legislation in the following areas: a) local economic development; b) urban and rural planning; c) land use and development; d) implementation of building regulations and building control standards; e) local environmental protection; f) provision and maintenance of public services and utilities, including water supply, sewers and drains, sewage treatment, waste management, local roads, local transport, and local heating schemes; g) local emergency response; h) provision of public pre-primary, primary and secondary education, including registration and licensing of educational institutions, recruitment, payment of salaries and training of education instructors and administrators; i) promotion and protection of human rights; j) provision of public primary health care; k) provision of family and other social welfare services, such as care for the vulnerable, foster care, child care, elderly care, including registration and licensing of these care centers, recruitment, payment of salaries and training of social welfare professionals; l) public housing; m) public health; n) licensing of local services and facilities, including those related to entertainment, cultural and leisure activities, food, lodging, markets, street vendors, local public transportation and taxis; o) naming of roads, streets and other public places; p) provision and maintenance of public parks and spaces; q) tourism; r) cultural and leisure activities; s) any matter which is not explicitly excluded from their competence nor assigned to any other authority.[10] Delegated Competencies. Central authorities in Republic of Kosovo shall delegate responsibility over the following competencies to municipalities, in accordance with the law: a) cadastral records; b) civil registries; c) voter registration; d) business registration and licensing; e) distribution of social assistance payments (excluding pensions); and f) forestry protection on the municipal territory within the authority delegated by the central authority, including the granting of licenses for the felling of trees on the basis of rules adopted by the Government. Central authorities in Republic of Kosovo may delegate other competencies to municipalities, as appropriate, in accordance with the law. Delegated competencies must in all cases be accompanied by the necessary funding in compliance with objectives, standards and requests determined by the Government of Kosovo.[11]

11. Enhanced Municipal Competencies

Municipalities explained below shall have their own competencies enhanced in the areas of health, education and cultural affairs and shall have participatory right in selecting local station police commanders as set forth in the subsequent articles. Central authorities of Republic of Kosovo shall monitor the exercise of enhanced competencies, in accordance with the central legislation providing for equal access to public 8 services; minimum quality and quantity standards in the provision of public services; minimum qualifications of personnel and training facilities; general principles on licensing and accreditation of public service providers. Municipalities exercising enhanced municipal competencies may cooperate with any other municipality in providing services.[12] Enhanced Competencies in Secondary Health Care The municipalities of Mitrovicë/ North, Graçanicë/Gracanica, Shtërpcë / Štrpce shall have the competence for provision of secondary health care, including registration and licensing of health care institutions, recruitment, payment of salaries and training of health care personnel and administrators; Enhanced Competencies in the University Education. The municipality of Mitrovicë/ Mitrovica North shall have competence for the provision of higher education, including registration and licensing of educational institutions, recruitment, payment of salaries and Enhanced Competencies in the Area of Culture All municipalities in which the Kosovo Serb Community is in the majority have authority to exercise responsibility for cultural affairs, including, protection and

---

[10] Law for Local Self-Governance of Republic of Kosovo
[11] Law for Local Self-Governance of Republic of Kosovo
[12] Law for Local Self-Governance of Republic of Kosovo

13

promotion of Serbian and other religious and cultural heritage within the municipal territory as well as support for local religious communities in accordance with the applicable law[13]. Municipalities may cooperate with any other municipality in cultural affairs. Education instructors and administrators. Enhanced Participatory Rights in Selection of the Local Police Station Commanders Municipalities in which Kosovo Serb community is in a majority shall exercise enhanced participatory rights in the selection of the local station police commanders in accordance with law on police.

12. Basic Principles of Municipal Finances

Municipalities have their own budgets and finances to finance and implement their competencies. The municipal budget consist of own source revenues; grants from the Government of Republic of Kosovo; donations and other revenues. Municipal budget and finance are regulated by a law on local finance. Basic public financial management and accountability requirements set out in the central legislation shall apply to all municipalities.[14]

13. Public Utilities Provided by Municipal Enterprises.

Where local public utilities are provided by municipal enterprises the enterprises have submit their budgets to the Municipal Assembly for approval. The budget proposals have include a proposed tariff structure for the provision of services and has submitted before 15 November in the year before the next fiscal year. Where an enterprise provides local public utilities for more than one municipality, arrangements shall be made by the municipalities to establish a join management Board and the manner of the oversight of the Board.

14. Internal Audit

Municipalities have the legal obligation to perform an internal audit at least once a year. According to law article 26.2. [15] Municipalities s have the right to establish an autonomous in-house audit service or ensure internal auditing by an audit firm accredited in accordance with the applicable legislation of Republic of Kosovo.[16]

15. External Audit

---

[13] Law for Local Self-Governance of Republic of Kosovo , Article 22.1
[14] Law for Local Self-Governance of Republic of Kosovo
[15] Law for Local Self-Governance of Republic of Kosovo
16

14

A central autonomous authority shall perform external audits of each municipality on annual basis in accordance with the applicable law on the Auditor General of Republic of Kosovo. Each auditor's report and the replies of municipal authorities should be made public.[17]

16.Cooperation between Municipalities of Republic of Kosovo

Municipalities have the right to cooperate and form partnerships with other Republic of Kosovo municipalities within their areas of competence to carry out functions of mutual interest, 10 based upon the principles of European Chart for Local Self-Government and in accordance with the law.

17. Municipal Partnerships

Municipal responsibilities in the areas of their own and enhanced competencies with the exception of those listed under paragraph 2 Article 40 of this law may be exercised through municipal partnerships. The activities of the partnerships shall also be funded through the municipal budgets of the participating municipalities. Such partnerships may take all actions necessary to implement and exercise their functional cooperation through inter alia, the establishment of a decision making body comprised of representatives appointed by the assemblies of the participating municipalities, the hiring and dismissal of administrative and advisory personnel, and decisions on funding and other operational needs of the partnership. Municipal decisions on the activities of the partnerships shall be subject to the mandatory review of legality in accordance with the provisions of Article 79 of law[18].

18.Cross-Border Cooperation of Municipalities

Municipalities shall have the right to enter into cooperative agreements with foreign local self-government bodies in all areas of own municipal competencies and enhanced competencies with the exception those listed in paragraph 2 Article 40 of this law. Municipalities shall be entitled to cooperate, within the areas of their own competencies, with municipalities and institutions, including government agencies, in the Republic of Serbia.[19] Such cooperation may take the form of the provision by Serbian institutions of financial and technical assistance,

---

[17] Law for Local Self-Governance of Republic of Kosovo
[18] Law for Self- Local governance
[19] Law for Local Self-Governance of Republic of Kosovo

including expert personnel and equipment, in the implementation of municipal competencies. Municipalities shall notify the ministry responsible for the local government in advance of any intention to engage in cross-border cooperation. The notification shall include the draft cooperation agreement between the municipalities and proposed counterparts. The draft cooperation agreement shall set out the following elements: a) names of parties intending to enter into agreement; b) intended effective date of the agreement; c) envisaged areas and objectives of cooperation; and d) modalities for the provision of staff and equipment, the level of funding and the funding processing mechanism and procedural arrangement, in accordance with public financial management requirements applicable to all municipalities. Following the review of the draft agreement, the ministry responsible for local government may enjoin amendments to the draft cooperation agreement, or, if it considers that a breach of the law cannot be remedied otherwise, the ministry may suspend the intended cooperation[20]. The municipality may challenge such action of the ministry in the District Court competent for the territory of the municipality. Partnerships between Republic of Kosovo municipalities shall be entitled to direct relations with institutions in the Republic of Serbia only to the extent necessary to implement practical activities of the partnership. Right of Municipalities to Associate For the protection and promotion of their common interests, municipalities may form and belong to associations that operate in conformity with the law.[21]

19. Associations of Municipalities of Republic of Kosovo

Individual municipalities may join representative associations of local self-government bodies of Republic of Kosovo.[22] The incorporating acts and financial documents of such associations shall be made public. Participating municipalities shall make public the information about the activity of such associations and their budgetary contributions to the associations. Such associations may offer to its members a number of services, including training, capacity building, technical assistance as well as research on municipal competencies and policy recommendation in accordance with law.[23]

International Associations of Local Government Associations of Republic of Kosovo municipalities may cooperate with international associations of local authorities.

---

[20] Law for Self- Local Governance, Article 30.5
[21] Law for Local Self-Governance of Republic of Kosovo
[22] Law for Local Self-Governance of Republic of Kosovo
[23] Law for Local Self-Governance of Republic of Kosovo

20. Villages, Settlements and Urban Quarters

Each municipality may make arrangements with villages, settlements and urban quarters within its territory to ensure that the services are offered closer to all citizens of the municipality. With the approval of the municipality, villages, settlements and urban quarters, singly or in combination, may carry out activities that are within the responsibilities and powers of the municipality. In this event, municipalities shall provide sufficient resources to the villages, settlements and urban quarters.

The ministry responsible for the local government shall issue instructions on the arrangements between the municipality and villages, settlements and urban quarters. The Statute and local municipal regulations shall stipulate the form of co-operation between the municipality and villages, settlements and urban quarters and the scope of work and organization of villages, settlements and urban quarters. All villages, settlements and urban quarters shall comply with the applicable law when carrying out activities by arrangement with the municipality.

21. Municipal Assembly

Municipal Assembly is the highest representative body of the municipality and shall be directly elected by the citizens in accordance with the Law on Local Elections and procedures.[24] All citizens of the Municipality may stand for in the Municipal Assembly provided they meet the requirements as set forth in the Law on Local Elections.[25] The mandate of the each members of the Municipal Assembly shall be verified by a commission on verification of mandates established by the Municipal Assembly before the signing of the mandate by each member. All members of the Municipal Assembly shall subscribe to the following solemn oath or declaration of office: "I swear (or solemnly declare) that I will perform my duties and exercise my powers as a member of the Municipal Assembly of municipality honorably, faithfully, impartially, conscientiously and according to law, so as to ensure conditions for a peaceful life for all citizens. Members of the Municipal Assembly who fail to subscribe to the oath or the signing of the mandate in accordance with law within one month of the certification of the election results shall cease to be a member.[26]

---

[24] Election Law in Kosovo
[25] Law for Local Self-Governance of Republic of Kosovo
[26] Law for Local Self-Governance of Republic of Kosovo

22.Number and Election of Assembly Members

The number of members in the Municipal Assembly of a Municipality shall be proportional, dependent upon the number of citizens in the Municipality. a) if a Municipality has up to 10.000 citizens, the Assembly for that Municipality shall consist of 15 members; b) if a Municipality has from 10.001 to 20.000 citizens, the Assembly for that Municipality shall consist of 19 members; c) if a Municipality has from 20.001 to 30.000 citizens, the Assembly for that Municipality shall consist of 21 members; d) if a Municipality has from 30.001 to 50.000 citizens, the Assembly for that Municipality shall consist of 27 members; e) if a Municipality has from 50.001 to 70.000 citizens, the Assembly for that Municipality shall consist of 31 members; f) if a Municipality has from 70.001 to 100.000 citizens, the Assembly for that Municipality shall consist of 35 members; g) if a Municipality has more than 100.000 citizens, the Assembly for that Municipality shall consist of 41 members. The municipal assembly of the Pristina shall consist of 51 members.[27]

23.Term of Office: The term of office of members of the Municipal Assembly shall be four years. A member of the Municipal Assembly shall cease to be a member: a) at the expiration of the member's term of office; b) at the change of the municipality of the residence where he is elected; c) upon the submission of a written resignation of his post to the Mayor of the Municipality; d) if a member is convicted of a criminal offence by a final court decision; e) if he/she misses Municipal Assembly meetings for three (3) consecutive months without valid excuse; or, f) if this law, or other laws applicable to the member, disqualifies or deems ineligible the member. A member of a municipal assembly may not simultaneously hold a position of a member of the Assembly of Republic of Kosovo.[28]

24. Conflicts of Interest

A member of the Municipal Assembly or of a committee shall be excluded from the decision-making and administrative procedures relating to any matter in which he or she, or an immediate family member of his or hers, has a personal or financial interest according to law. [29] Each member is required to disclose all conflicts of interest immediately as they arise at any meeting at which the member is present. Any member may supply information about the interests of another

---

[27] Law for Local Self-Governance of Republic of Kosovo
[28] Law for Local Self-Governance of Republic of Kosovo
[29] Law for Local Self-Governance of Republic of Kosovo

member. Before the first meeting of the Municipal Assembly, members of the Assembly shall record a full and open statement of their financial interests in a public register to be kept by an authorized officer of the municipality. Members shall record any change in their financial interests as they occur[30].

The Statute and Rules of Procedure shall set out the measures to be taken to exclude members from the decision-making and administrative procedures where they have a conflict of interest.

25.Rights and Duties of Municipal Assembly Members

All members of the Municipal Assembly they have fair and equal rights and opportunities to participate fully in the proceedings of the Assembly. The Municipal Assembly shall ensure that these rights and opportunities are provided in its Statute and Rules of Procedure. A member of the Municipal Assembly may request information concerning municipal matters from the Mayor, or the chairperson of a committee. The request shall be dealt with in accordance with procedures to be set out in the Statute and Rules of Procedure. A member of the Municipal Assembly may submit remarks in writing form , which shall be attached to the minutes. A member of the Municipal Assembly may address, but not vote at meetings of any committee of the Municipal Assembly of which he or she is not a member. He or she may propose to the chairperson of the committee that any matter which is the responsibility of the committee should be discussed. A member of the Municipal Assembly may request from the Mayor information necessary for his work as a member.[31] If he or she is dissatisfied with the response he or she may raise the issue with the Municipal Assembly. A member of the Municipal Assembly shall be allowed to be absent from their workplace for such periods as are reasonably necessary for Assembly business. The Municipal Assembly shall, in accordance with the Statute of the Municipality and guidelines issued by the central government, compensate members of the Municipal Assembly[32]. It is the duty of the members of the Municipal Assembly to attend all validly called meetings of the Municipal Assembly and any committees in which they are members, unless justifiable reasons for their absence exist.[33]

25. Operation of Municipal Assembly

---

[30] Law for Self- Local Governance, Article 38.3
[31] Law for Local Self-Governance of Republic of Kosovo
[32] Law for Self- Local Governance, Article 39.6
[33] Law for Local Self-Governance of Republic of Kosovo

The municipal assembly operates on the basis of this law, the Statute and other sub-legal acts. The Municipal Assembly may not delegate its responsibility for decisions concerning: a) statute or the Rules of Procedure, municipal regulations and the adoption, amendment or repeal thereof; b) the approval of the budget and investment plans; c) the approval of other financial matters that are reserved to the Assembly by the Statute or the Rules of Procedure; 15 d) the annual work plan and annual report; e) the establishment of the committees required by the present Law; f) the election of the Chairperson and Deputy Chairperson of the Municipal Assembly; g) the level of fees and charges; h) the creation and use, in accordance with applicable legislation, of municipal symbols, decorations and honorary titles; i) the naming and renaming of roads, streets and other public places; j) he making of inter-municipal and intra-municipal agreements; k) the making of decisions to join representative associations of municipalities of Republic of Kosovo and l) other responsibilities that are required by law. The Municipal Assembly may delegate the power to make other decisions to a committee of the Municipal Assembly or to the Mayor of the municipality. The Municipal Assembly may withdraw the delegation at any time

26.The Chairperson of the Municipal Assembly

The Municipal Assembly shall elect the Chairperson of the Municipal Assembly from among the members. The Chairperson of the Municipal Assembly shall be elected for the same term of office as the Assembly members. Voting for the Chairperson of the Municipal Assembly shall be by secret ballot.[34] To be elected on the first ballot, a candidate must receive the vote of the more than half of the total number of elected members.[35] If no candidate has received the required majority on the first ballot, then two candidates with the majority of votes will go to a second ballot. Candidate who receives more than half of the votes of the total number of elected members shall be elected the Chairperson of the Municipal Assembly.[36]

27. Inaugural Session

The Municipal Assembly shall hold its inaugural meeting within fifteen (15) days from the day of the election results certification. The inaugural meeting of the Municipal Assembly shall be called by the Mayor (where elected) within fifteen

---

[34] Law for Local Self-Governance of Republic of Kosovo
[35] Law for Local Self-Governance of Republic of Kosovo
[36] Law for Local Self-Governance of Republic of Kosovo

(15) days from day that the election results are certified[37]. If the Mayor fails to call a meeting as per his/her duty in paragraph 2 of this Article, the inaugural meeting of the Municipal Assembly may be called by the oldest elected member of the Municipal Assembly within fifteen (15) days of the Mayor's failure to call the inaugural meeting of the Municipal Assembly[38].

If the oldest member of the Assembly fails to call a meeting as per his duty in paragraph 3 of this Article, the inaugural meeting of the Municipal Assembly may be constituted upon the initiative of the majority of the elected members of the Municipal Assembly. Meetings of the Municipal Assembly held before the election of the Chairperson of the Municipal Assembly shall be chaired by the oldest elected member of the Municipal Assembly present in the meeting.

28. Meetings of Municipal Assembly

The Chairperson of the Municipal Assembly shall call and chair the meetings of the Municipal Assembly. The Municipal Assembly shall hold at least ten sessions per year five of which should take place during the first six months of year, as specified by the Rules of Procedure. All the members of the Municipal Assembly shall be given written notice, as required, at least seven (7) working days prior to the meeting. Such notice shall include: a) the date of the meeting; b) the time of the meeting; c) the place of the meeting; d) the agenda for the meeting; and e) materials of the meeting. f) Other data as may be determined by the statute or rule of procedure. The notice and the meeting materials shall respect the Law on Languages. The same notice shall be announced to the public. The notice from paragraphs 3 and 4 of this Article shall also be sent to ministry responsible for the local government.

29. Extraordinary Meetings of Municipal Assembly

An extraordinary meeting of the Municipal Assembly shall be called by the Chairperson or upon a written request of at least one third of the total number of members of the Municipal Assembly or of the Mayor.[39] The right to call an extraordinary meeting shall also include the right set the agenda for the meeting called.[40] The items of the agenda for the extraordinarily called meetings may not

---

[37] Law for Self- Local Governance, Article,42.2
[38] Law for Self- Local Governance, Article 42.3
[39] Law for Local Self-Governance of Republic of Kosovo
[40] Law for Local Self-Governance of Republic of Kosovo

be changed at such a meeting. An extraordinary meeting of the Municipal Assembly shall not be held unless all members of the Municipal Assembly and the public are given written notice, as required in the rules of procedure, at least three (3) working days prior to the date of the meeting.[41]

The same procedural requirements for the notice and other issues applicable to the regular meetings shall also apply to extraordinary meetings. The procedures set out above shall not apply to meetings called because of urgent circumstances.

29.1 Open Meetings

Meetings of the Municipal Assembly and all its committees are open to the public opinions. Members of the public are permitted to follow and participate in meetings of the Municipal Assembly in the manner specified in the Rules of Procedure. A notice of the meeting of the Municipal Assembly shall be made public. The Municipal Assembly or the committee may by a majority vote decide to exclude the public from the whole or a part of a meeting when an open meeting: a) might lead to public disorder or violence; b) would threaten to disclose information [and documents] to the disclosure of which is restricted in accordance with the Law on Access to Official Documents, c) would threaten to disclose personally or commercially sensitive information; or d) would threaten to disclose information about actual or imminent court proceedings. In such event, a notice shall be given by the Municipal Assembly as to the decisions taken. Municipal Assembly may regulate by the Statute establish the rules the procedures for the holding of closed sessions.[42]

29.2. Quorum

The quorum for all meetings of the Municipal Assembly and its committees shall be at least one-half of all the members of Municipal Assembly or of its committees. The quorum shall be verified before any decision is taken.

29.3. Agenda

The agenda for a meeting of the Municipal Assembly shall be set by the Chairperson of the Municipal Assembly upon the agreement of the Mayor of

---

[41] Law for Local Self-Governance of Republic of Kosovo
[42] Law for Local Self-Governance of Republic of Kosovo

Municipality. A member of the Municipal Assembly may request to add an item to the agenda during a regular session of the Municipal Assembly if the matter sought to be included in the agenda is an urgent matter of public importance. Such a request shall be approved or rejected by a majority vote. The Rules of Procedure of the Municipal Assembly shall set out further provisions for the preparation, approval, and amendments to the agenda.

29.4. Voting

At all meetings of the Municipal Assembly and its committees, each member including the chairperson shall have one vote, but the chairperson shall have an additional casting vote if an equal number of votes are cast for and against a proposal. Unless otherwise explicitly provided for in this law, decisions of the Municipal Assembly or of a committee shall be adopted by the majority of the members present and voting. Abstentions shall be noted for the purpose of establishing the quorum, but shall not otherwise be taken into account for the voting results.[43]

Minutes shall be taken of all meetings of the Municipal Assembly and its committees and shall be approved at the next meeting in accordance with the Law on the Use of Languages.[44]

30. Dissolving a Non-Functioning Municipal

If a municipal assembly fails to perform a mandatory function up to the standards set by law or becomes non-functioning, thus jeopardizing the exercise of basic rights of the citizens, the ministry responsible for the local government shall notify the failure to perform to the municipality and request that appropriate measures be taken in order to ensure the smooth performance of the challenged function as soon as possible according to the procedures it should be followed .[45]There are some legal moment important in some situation according to function of municipal institution such are cases stated in law: a municipality is considered as non-functioning if it: a) fails to elect a Chairperson thirty (30) days after it is duly constituted; b) fails to adopt its statute within sixty (60) days from the day it is duly constituted; c) fails to adopt the budget within the time limit determined by the law; or d) fails to hold a meeting for a period of more than six (6) months. The

---

[43] Law for Local Self-Governance of Republic of Kosovo
[44] Law for Local Self-Governance of Republic of Kosovo
[45] Law for Local Self-Governance of Republic of Kosovo

ministry responsible for the local government shall notify the Government of Republic of Kosovo on the non-functioning of municipality. The Government of Republic of Kosovo may dissolve a non-functioning Municipal Assembly. New elections will be held for the Municipal Assembly in accordance with the law on local election of Republic of Kosovo . Mandate of Municipal Assembly is 4 year with the possibilities for extraordinary election. There are some matter which make obstacles duo the function of municipal institutions especially when the Mayer of municipalities is elected directly by citizens and Municipality Assemblies are consist by different political parties , there are such a cases in Kosovo , when the Mayer is blocked because other political parties which have a great number in Assemblies they do not support Mayer or his decision.

31. Permanent Committees

The Municipal Assemblies shall establish and maintain the Committee on Policy and Finance and the Committee on Communities permanent committees which are very important for function of municipal institutions. The Municipal Assembly shall establish such committees as it deems necessary and appropriate to carry out its responsibilities. Unless specified otherwise in this law, committees shall reflect the composition of the Municipal Assembly.[46]

32. Policy and Finance Committee

The Policy and Finance Committee shall be chaired by the Chairperson of the Municipal Assembly and its composition shall reflect the representation of the political entities in the Municipal Assembly. The Policy and Finance Committee shall be responsible to review all the policy documents, strategic approach and fiscal and financial documents, plans, and initiatives including strategic planning documents, the annual Medium Term Budget Framework, the annual procurement plan, the annual regulation on taxes, fees and charges, the annual internal audit work plan, the annual medium term budget and any changes to the budget during a fiscal year as well as reports from the Mayor and submit recommendations for action to the Municipal As Communities Committee.[47] The membership of the Communities Committee shall include the members of the Municipal Assembly and community representatives. Any community living in the municipality shall be represented by at least one representative in the Communities Committee.[48] The

---

[46] Law for Local Self-Governance of Republic of Kosovo
[47] Law for Local Self-Governance of Republic of Kosovo
[48] Law for Local Self-Governance of Republic of Kosovo

representatives of communities shall comprise the majority of the Communities Committee. The Communities Committee shall be responsible to review compliance of the municipal authorities with the applicable law and review all municipal policies, documents, projects , practices and activities related with the aim to ensure that rights and interests of the Communities are fully respected and shall recommend to the Municipal Assembly measures it considers appropriate to ensure the implementation of provisions related to the need of communities to promote, express, preserve and develop their ethnic, cultural, religious and linguistic identities, as well as to ensure adequate protection of the rights of communities within the municipality.

33. Deputy Chairperson for Communities

In municipalities where at least ten per cent (10%) of the citizens belong to Communities not in the majority in those municipalities, a post of the Chairperson of the Municipal Assembly for Communities shall be reserved for a representative of these communities. The post of the Deputy Chairperson of the Municipal Assembly for Communities is held by the non-majority community's candidate who received the most votes on the open list of candidates for election to the Municipal Assembly.[i]

34. Duties of the Deputy Chairperson of a Municipality for Communities

The Deputy Chairperson of a Municipality for Communities shall promote inter-community dialogue and serve as formal focal point for addressing non-majority communities' concerns and interests in meetings of the Assembly and its work. The Deputy Chairperson of a Municipality for Communities shall be responsible for reviewing claims by communities or their members that the acts or decisions of the municipal assembly violate their constitutionally guaranteed rights. The Deputy Chairperson of a Municipality for Communities shall refer such matters to the Municipal Assembly for its reconsideration of the act or decision. In the event the Municipal Assembly chooses not to reconsider its act or decision, or the Deputy Chairperson of a Municipality for Communities deems that even upon reconsideration the act or decision presents a violation of a constitutionally guaranteed right, the Deputy Chairperson of a Municipality for Communities may submit the matter directly to the Constitutional Court, which may decide whether to accept the matter for review.

35. Election of the Mayor of the Municipality

The Mayor of the Municipality shall be elected by a direct election in accordance with the law on local elections. The Mayor of the Municipality shall be elected for a term of four years. The term of office of the Mayor of the Municipality shall end upon: a) the completion of his mandate; b) his death; c) his resignation; d) his change of residence to another municipality; e) his failure to report on duty for more than 1 month without a valid reason. f) His removal from office in accordance with this law; g) a final court decision depriving the Mayor of legal capacity to act; or h) his conviction of a criminal offence with an order for imprisonment for six (6) months or more.

35.1. Oath of Office

Upon election, the Municipal Mayor shall subscribe to a solemn oath or declaration of office before the members of the Municipal Assembly. The form of the oath of office shall be as follows: "I swear (or solemnly declare) that I will perform my duties and exercise my powers as Mayor of … municipality honorably, faithfully, impartially, conscientiously and according to law, so as to ensure conditions for a peaceful and prosperous life for all. The Mayor who fails to subscribe to the oath within one (1) month of the certification of the election results shall forfeit his term.

35.2. Responsibilities of the Mayor

The Mayor shall execute the following responsibilities: a) represents and acts on behalf of the Municipality; b) leads the municipal government and its administration and conducts the financial administration of the municipality; c) exercises all competencies not explicitly assigned to the Municipal Assembly or its committees. d) executes the Municipal Assembly acts; e) appoints and dismisses his deputies; f) appoints and dismiss his advisors who assist him in discharging his duties; g) organizes the work and directs the policy of the municipality; h) proposes municipal regulations and other acts for the approval of Municipal Assembly; i) proposes municipal development, regulatory and investments plans; proposes the annual budget for the approval of the Municipal Assembly and executes the budget adopted; j) reports before the Municipal Assembly on the economic-financial situation and the implementation of the investment plans of the Municipality at least once every six months or as often as required by the Municipal Assembly; and k) may request the Municipal Assembly only once to review a municipal act when he deems the act to violate the applicable legislation and/or the interests of communities. l) shall consult the Deputy Mayor for

Communities about the matters related to non-majority communities; and m) other activities assigned to him/her by the statute.

35.3. Conflicts of Interest

As soon as possible following his/her election, the Mayor shall terminate any contract or association that may call into question her/his ability to carry out his/her responsibilities fairly and impartially. The Mayor shall be excluded from decision-making and administrative procedures relating to any matter in which he/she, or an immediate family member of his or hers, has a personal or financial interest. The Mayor shall be required to disclose all conflicts of interest immediately as they arise. The Mayor may voluntarily exclude himself/herself from decision-making and administrative procedures if he/she considers that they may have a conflict of interest. The Municipal Mayor shall record any change in their financial interests as soon as it occurs. The Statute shall set out the measures to be taken to exclude the Municipal Mayor from the decision-making and administrative procedures where they have a conflict of interest.

35.4. Deputy Mayor of a Municipality

In each municipality, the Mayor shall have one Deputy Mayor. The Deputy Mayor of Municipality is appointed by the Mayor for the same term of office as the Mayor and may be dismissed from office by the Mayor. Upon Mayor's request, the Deputy Mayor shall assist the Mayor in discharging his daily executive functions and shall act on behalf of the Mayor in her/his absence. When the post of the Deputy Mayor becomes vacant, the Mayor shall appoint a new one no later than thirty days after the vacancy arises. The Article 60 on the conflict on interest of the Mayor shall apply mutatis mutandis to the Deputy Mayor[49].

35.5. Deputy Mayor for Communities

There shall be a Deputy Mayor for Communities in those municipalities where at least 10% of the citizens belong to non-majority communities. The Deputy Mayor for Communities shall be elected for the same term of office as the Mayor.The appointment and dismissal of the Deputy Mayor for Communities shall be proposed by the Mayor and shall get approval of the majority of the municipal assembly members present and voting and the majority of the municipal assembly members present and voting belonging to the non-majority communities.

---

[49] Law for Local Self-Governance ,Article 60

The deputy mayor for communities shall assist the Mayor and provide him/her advice and guidance to the Mayor on issues related to the non-majority communities. When the post of the Deputy Mayor becomes vacant, the Mayor shall appoint a new one no later than thirty days after the vacancy arises according to the procedures of paragraph 3 of this Article. 61.6 The Article 59 on the conflict on interest of the Mayor shall apply mutatis mutandis to the Deputy Mayor for Communities.

36. Municipal Directors

The municipal administration shall be organized into directorates. Each municipal directorate is managed by a director who is employed and dismissed by the Mayor. The directors manage their directorates in accordance with the strategic and political strategies of Mayor and in accordance with Laws and municipal applicable regulations. Directors shall regularly report to the Mayor for the matters that are under their responsibility and shall provide him/her all necessary information and reports for the decision-making process.

36.1. Conflicts of Interest for Directors

Directors shall be excluded from the decision-making and administrative procedures relating to any matter in which he or she, or an immediate family member of his or hers, has a personal or financial interest. Directors are required to present in written any conflict of interest immediately after such conflict arises. The statute and rule of procedure includes the measures that should be taken to exclude directors from the decision-making and administrative procedures where they have a conflict of interest.

36.2. Removal from the Office

Municipal Mayor may be suspended from the office by a decision of the Government of Republic of Kosovo within thirty (30) days, if it considers that the Mayor has violated the Constitution and the applicable laws. If the ministry responsible for local government considers that the conditions for the suspension of the Municipal Mayor are met, it shall recommend the suspension of such Mayor to 24 the Government of Republic of Kosovo. The Government of Republic of Kosovo may suspend the Municipal Mayor (for up to 30 day) by a decision and submit the case to the Constitutional Court. If the Constitutional Court upholds the decision; the Government shall remove the Mayor from the office.

36.3. Municipal Civil Service

The municipal civil service shall consist of all the persons employed by a municipal authority whose salary is paid by the Budget of Republic of Kosovo except: a) mayor, deputy mayor/s and municipal directors; b) chairperson, deputy chairperson/s and all the members of Municipal Assembly; Municipal directors, directors of institutions and enterprises under the authority of the municipality and the civil servants of the administration of the municipality shall not be members of the Assembly of Republic of Kosovo or of the municipal assembly of the municipality where they work. Elections for a Municipal Assembly shall not constitute a cause for reconsidering appointments of civil servants.

36.4. Municipal Administration and the Head of Personnel.

The municipal administration shall be organized into directorates. Each municipal directorate is managed by a director. Municipal Directors shall be employed and dismissed by the Mayor. The municipal administration shall have a Head of Personnel. The Mayor shall announce the post, recruitment and dismissal of the Head of Personnel in accordance with the applicable law on civil service. If the position of the Head of Personnel becomes vacant, the Mayor shall appoint in an acting capacity a senior member of the municipal civil service. Within sixty (60) days, the Mayor shall recruit a new Head in accordance with above.

36.5. Public Information and Consultation

Each municipality shall hold periodically, at least twice a year, a public meeting at which any person or organization with an interest in the municipality may participate. The date and place of the meeting shall be publicized at least two weeks in advance. One of the meetings shall be held during the first six months of the year. At the meeting municipal representatives shall inform participants about the activities of the municipality and participants may ask questions and make proposals to the elected representatives of the municipality. In addition to the public meetings noted above, Municipalities are obliged to inform the citizens of the Municipality of any important plans or programs of public interest, which shall be regulated by the Municipal Statute. The Municipal Assembly shall adopt municipal regulation promoting the transparency of the legislative, executive and administrative bodies of the municipalities, enhancing the public participation in the decision making at the local level, and facilitating the public access to official documents of the municipalities. The ministry responsible for local government may issue administrative instructions on municipal transparency. Any person may inspect any document held by the Municipality, unless such disclosure is restricted in accordance with the Law on Access to Official Documents.

36.6. Right of Petition

Any person or organization with an interest in the municipality shall have the right to present a petition to the Municipal Assembly about any matter relating to the responsibilities and powers of the municipality. The Municipal Assembly shall consider the petition in accordance with its Statute and Rules of Procedure.

36.7. Citizens' Initiative

The citizens may take initiative to propose regulations, within the competencies of the municipality, for adoption by assembly or by a vote of the citizens in accordance with the applicable law. The proponents shall submit a draft of the proposed regulation to the Chairperson of the Municipal Assembly. 70.3. The draft regulation proposed shall be signed by 15% of the registered voters for consideration by the Municipal Assembly. The Municipal Assembly is obliged to consider the proposed the regulation and take action upon it within 60 days of the receipt.

37. Referendum

The citizens of a municipality may request that a regulation of the Municipal Assembly adopted by the Municipal Assembly, be submitted to a referendum by the citizens. The request must be submitted to the Chairperson of the Municipal Assembly within 30 days from the date of adoption of the regulation and must be signed by 10% of the registered voters. The Municipal Assembly shall consider and act upon the request within the thirty days after the receipt of a valid petition in accordance with applicable law.

37.1. Recall of the Mayor

The citizens of a municipality may take the initiative to remove a mayor from the office. A request to this effect shall be signed by twenty (20) percent of the registered voters and shall be submitted to the Chairperson of Municipal Assembly who shall refer the matter to the appropriate institution for the administration of voting. If the majority of the registered voters vote in favor of the Mayor's removal, new mayoral elections shall take place in accordance with the law on elections.

37.2. Consultative Committees

The Municipal Assembly have consultative committees within sectors for the purpose of enabling citizen participation in the decision making process. The membership of the committees have include citizens and representatives of nongovernmental organizations. The consultative committees may submit proposals, conduct research and provide opinions on municipal assembly initiatives in accordance with the Municipal Statute.

37.3. Objectives of the Administrative Review

The administrative review of the municipalities has the following objectives: a) to strengthen the ability of the local self-government bodies to fulfill their responsibilities through advice, support, and assistance; b) to ensure the lawfulness of the activities of local self-government bodies; and c) to ensure that the rights and interest of citizens are respected.

37.4. Basic Principles of the Administrative Review

The administrative review of municipalities shall only be exercised in accordance with Constitution and law. No prior review can be exercised unless otherwise provided by this law. Administrative review shall have as minimal as possible impact on the interests of local self-government and may not limit the right of local authorities to manage the affairs falling in the scope of their powers in accordance with the law. The intervention of the supervisory authority shall be proportional to the importance of the interests which it intends to protect.

37. Supervisory Authorities

The ministry responsible for the local government is the supervisory authority unless; the responsibility for the review of municipalities is assigned by law to the responsible ministry or institution with respect to a specific field. The review of the delegated competencies is exercised by the body of central government which has delegated them

37.6. Mutual Responsibilities in the Process of Administrative Review

Municipal and supervisory authorities are obliged to cooperate with each other in the process of administrative review. All measures of review shall be taken by review authorities through the relevant legal acts. Such acts shall state the legal basis and explain the reasons for the application of a certain review measure.

37.7. Rights of Supervisory Authorities to be informed

The supervisory authority has the right to receive and obtain full information on all matters concerned, including the right to visit the municipal offices and municipal facilities and to request access to municipal documents. The Mayor shall be responsible for making this information available to the supervisory body. During such visits, the representatives of the supervisory body shall not give direct instructions to the staff of the local self-government bodies. Any request for documents shall be addressed to the local government body and the transmission of the documents shall be ensured by the Mayor in accordance with paragraph 1 of Article 77 of this Law[50]. The ministry responsible for the local government has the right to be regularly informed by the municipalities on the areas of which the ministry it is not the supervisory authority.

37.8. Types of Review

Review over the operation of municipalities in the area of own and enhanced competencies shall be limited to review of the legality. The administrative review over the operation of municipalities in the area of delegated competences shall include review of the legality and expediency of actions.

37.9. Regular Review of Legality

The Mayor of a municipality shall forward to the supervisory authority by the 10th of each month, a list of all acts adopted by the Mayor and the Assembly in the previous month. The supervisory authority shall have the right to supervise any act, which had not been controlled under the procedure of mandatory review, within 30 days upon the receipt of the list mentioned in paragraph 1 of this Article.

40. Mandatory Review of Legality

The following acts shall be subject to the procedure of mandatory review of legality; a) general acts adopted by the municipal assemblies; b) decisions related to the joining and activities of the cooperative partnerships; c) acts adopted within

---

[50] Law for Self-Governance of republic of Kosovo , Article 77

the framework of the implementation delegated competencies. All municipalities are obliged to submit to the supervisory body all aforementioned acts within 7 days from the day of issuance. The acknowledgement of receipt by the supervisory body on the submitted act of the local government body is certified through its registration in the protocol office of the supervisory body. Supervisory body is obliged to give its opinion on the legality of any registered act within 15 days from its receipt in accordance with the aforementioned procedures.

41. The Procedure for the Review of Legality

If the supervisory authority considers a decision or other act of a municipality to be inconsistent with the Constitution and laws, it may request that the municipality reexamine such decision or act. The request shall state the grounds of the alleged violation of the Constitution or law and shall not suspend the execution of the municipal decision or other act at issue. The municipal body shall respond to request for re-examination within 30 days of notification of receipt of such request. If the municipal body accepts the request for re-examination, it may suspend the execution of the contested decision or act pending the deliberation by the municipal authorities[51]. If the municipal body fails to respond within the deadline or rejects the request or upholds the contested decision or act, the supervisory authority may challenge the act in question in the District Court competent for the territory of the municipality within 30 days following the failure to respond, notification of the rejection or the upholding of the contested decision[52] The District Court may order, by interim measure the suspension of the application of the contested decision or act or other temporary acts in accordance with the applicable law.

42. Request for Preliminary Consultation

Prior to the issuance of an act, a municipal body may request consultation with a supervisory body. The request for preliminary consultations shall contain a draft of the act intended to be issued and the specific issue for which the advice of the supervisory body is requested with respect to the legality and/or reasonability of the act in question. Supervisory authority is obliged to respond in writing within 30 days after the receipt of the request.

42.1. Review of Expediency

---

[51] Law for Self-Governance of republic of Kosovo , Article 82.3
[52] Law for Self-Governance of republic of Kosovo , Article 82.5

The supervisory authority responsible for exercising review over the delegated competencies shall have the right to request, within 30 days of reception of a copy of the an act, that the municipal body modify or repeal the contested act on the basis of expediency considerations. If the municipal body fails to act accordingly, the supervisory body responsible for exercising review over the expediency may modify, replace the act or suspend the execution of a municipal decision or other act. The supervising authority shall inform the municipal body of such decision within five (5) days of adoption of the decision.

42.3. Complaints of citizens

The complaints of citizens against an administrative act of the municipal organs shall be reviewed in accordance with Law on Administrative Procedure.

42.4.Publicity of the Administrative Review

The ministry responsible or local government shall submit to the Government and to the Assembly of Republic of Kosovo, by the end of March of each year, an annual report about its activities relating to the review of municipalities carried out in the previous year up to the end of March each year[53]. The report shall be made available to the public.

Repeal of Previous Legislation upon the entry into force of this law all prior legislation governing the Law on Local Self-Government shall be abrogated.

Chapter Two

1. Association / Association of Serbian Municipalities in Kosovo- Legal Comments

Kosovo cannot allow in any variant executive powers that would mean conflicting with the Kosovo Constitution and the law on local self-government.

"The association should be merely a consultative mechanism for the development of local government, the type of a referral mechanism and developer. Any other given power would imply the risk of a country's constitutional reorganization, this is not acceptable. "

---

[53] Law for Self-Governance of republic of Kosovo , Article ,86.2

Lack of transparency for the Association is the main strategic game of the Kosovo Government, just as it has happened with all other agreements where something else is said and at the end of the dialogue are received painful compromises from Kosovo. Serbian political representatives and many Kosovo Serbs see the Association as a way to strengthen ties between Kosovo Serbs and Serbia without (much) interference from Pristina.

AKS is a political creature that is often unclear in the juridical field, a political creature, and the attempt is to escape the juridical plane to politically act as a coordinating mechanism, ie a political but obvious legal mechanism, this mechanism is not despite the fact that many people and politicians as well as international organizations adopt the notions of action within Kosovo's laws, in the context of attempts to clarify

1.2. Kosovo's constitution of the transitional type

Kosovo's constitution is a transitional-type constitution that co-exists and interacts with international organizations; it has some dilemmas around the country's sovereignty. The biggest challenge was its implementation in the north of the state of Kosovo.

There are persistent situations where politics is challenged to challenge the constitution of the state

This constitution is attempted to be challenged by everyday politics in the country, not knowing it or with other intentions the political parties tend to comment and interpret according to the interests of the daily bazaar, which puts dilemmas and suspicions that there is no such constitution, there is also people who do interpretations without knowing the interpretations, normal that everyone can interpret but only formally and legally only the Constitutional Court. Political entities seem to be its biggest offenders where no chapter in the constitutional court law foresees taking legal measures against political parties that violate the constitution of the state or act unconstitutionally, the Slovenian court also takes action against political entities that violate whether political entities that do not respect the constitution or violate it are derecognized from the register of political parties. There are also many other people in the anarchic chain that reigns in Kosovo who are not jurists or of antagonist and interlocutor, who consider that they are committing anarchy and violating its legal principles. The attempts have not stopped in recent times to put unnecessary dilemmas on the constitution from

2014 until today. The constitution is taking on all sorts of people even lawyers that day deal with the immovable property and in the evening go to Tv talk about the constitution but also many people who know what they do in their everyday life and what profession they have Political parties and some individuals have not hesitated to send to the Constitutional Court often for all the articles of the constitution, so it has been a constant effort to challenge and depreciate the constitution of the country, understood these things are done for appetites for political power ignoring the country's constitution. There have been parties so far that they have called the country's constitution a defective, indeed the constitution is of the transitional type and over half of it is described by Ahtisaari's plan there are many linguistic errors, which clearly shows that the original text was drafted in English language the translation is rather weak, but there are many people who wanted and wanted to take the authorship without being part of the work of drafting the constitution or have been in the position of consultant, let us not forget that in the work of drafting the constitution I was myself, we were 15 experts divided into working groups where work documentation for the constitution and our proposals can be found in the prime minister's administration where the names of the members of the working group are preserved, some of it is taken from the comprehensive plan for the status of President Ahtisaari's Kosovo, and the rest is taken from the crane working pet, while being rounded up by international experts. Kosovo's constitution is generous enough that it allows the president to be nominated from outside the political parties that make up the assembly, but the political parties have so far chosen to take up this post despite the fact that the parliamentary system does not endorse a party president but president represents unity, however this post so far was coffers. Almost the Serbian plan or Serbian strategy has had some understanding in international circles and in the dialogue in Brussels. The international community has achieved its objectives by offering Kosovo independence while the Serbian minority have the maximum guaranteed rights almost equal to the majority Albanian majority in Kosovo and the maximum security and economic development of the north of the country through the fund for the north, then the judicial system in the north the state etc. It is no coincidence that such issues as the Constitution and the laws will change in the future, and it is not surprising, first of all, first of all the locals to change, or are encouraged to start changing the current Constitution not since it comes into force but why not first the international community to see what the interests of Kosovo's state institutions are to offer.

The test is done now can be expected or expected to be gathered comments from the Kosovo-Serbia agreement to approximate attitudes and once all has been done then to begin building a new Kosovo constitution, so far it was a transitional constitution so now it is necessary to be a new, more stable and timely constitution for the citizens. It was interesting and it sounded frivolous a meeting organized by Friedrich Erbert Stiftung two years ago, where some people talked about each one and gained personal merit of drafting Kosovo's constitutions historically, while the rest provided information and nothing else, the truth was Other, the constitutional framework was drafted by Dutch expert Lemon and his team, while other local people participated in consultative quality, made comments and remarks that were never part of the then constitutional framework or just some of the parts of that framework, as a result at that time resigned two local consultants, while the international community negotiated through diplomatic circles even with Serbian authorities not to forget the interest of Kosovo Serbs. This was the truth and the misfortune that neither then nor even now can we avoid.

It is interesting to mention other facts or other plans, since the current Constitution does not need to be changed because if the Kosovo Parliament approves the conclusions - "agreements" with Serbia, it is automatically applicable because the current Constitution clearly defines the priority of international agreements local laws although legally these agreements with Serbia are not international agreements but only conclusions between the two states. I think that this constitution as the highest legal and political act of the state despite the incomplete implementation in some parts of the state so in the north, and the implementation of some of its chapters in the part of the independent institutions and its mismanagement as well as some other articles so far it has reached the state of Kosovo to function properly, in the future there is a need for reform of this constitution, but better as they said the sooner the better. Free interpretation for: "Marriage of the Association of Serbian Municipalities"

Summary of Facts:

Kosovo has a constitutional order based on the two currently-guided formulas:

a) sui generis formula

B) Affirmative Law for Minorities

If we use the methods to establish the legality of the legal norm or the Latin "ratio of the leg" through the use of interpretations in this situation, we will take the truth of the norms of this agreement as follows: we should use linguistic interpretation in the original text in English, then it should be served with interpretations as follows: logical, evolutionary, purposeful and systematic. Based on the linguistic and logical interpretation of the constitution of the country the constitution - the part of the international conventions on human rights and the observance of these international conventions from Kosovo the assumption of obligations hence the embrace of the formula: affirmative European law and constitutional articles as follows: Chapter II Article 21, Article 22, Article 23, Article 24, 26, based on Article 124 of the Constitution, are also issued the following laws: Law on Local Self-Government, Law on Inter-Communal Cooperation, these laws derive from the European Charter for Local Self-Government accepting the affirmative affirmative formula for minorities and establishing a system of positive discrimination for minorities as an integral part of its constitution. The "agreement" for the "association" is built based on the 2013 agreement ratified in the Kosovo Assembly. Kosovo's constitution is transitory and in difficulty offers modern approaches to interpretation and quality standards that must have a modern and contemporary constitution. Kosovo has a sensitive or tangible constitution for respecting contemporary standards and has transitional norms. The association is an undefined body with defective definition based on logical interpretation and that intentional interpretation emerges as an uncompleted and non-finalized institution, its legal status should be defined to clarify its work and it is just an administrative body.

The agreement is in accordance with Article 19.2 of the Constitution (citation ratified international agreements and legally binding norms of international law prevail over international laws (the Association Agreement is in line with the 19 April 2013 agreement ratified by the Assembly of Kosovo. 1. Interpretation

1.3. Statute and Association:

"Association of Serbian Municipalities" (Use of the following interpretations: linguistic, evolutionary, intentional and systematic interpretation)

1. "Association of Serbian Municipalities" is a mechanism or administrative body with powers of oversight, coordination and development for the administrative areas mentioned in the following conclusions: social issues, education, health, economic development, spatial planning, environment and environment and do

not contradict Article 44.1 of the Constitution (freedom of association) and Article 124.4.

2. Oversight implies the effective implementation of the objectives of the association ie its statute act and decisions, common regulations. The issued acts are of a administrative nature. The Association also monitors the implementation of its objectives in the territory of municipalities that exercise some common competences. The Association may also exercise additional powers that may be delegated to it while maintaining the purpose of its establishment.

3.The Association provides administrative services in the areas designated for the citizens of these municipalities in accordance with the laws of Kosovo (Law on Local Self-Government and the Law on Inter-Municipal Cooperation and other laws.

4.The Association may enter into relations with associations of other local and international communes (Article 124, paragraph 4 of the constitution - inter-municipal and cross-border cooperation), as a "specific administrative body" (based on logical and intentional interpretation), can construct reports and other reports from the areas that are or may be delegated by the central authority.

5. To evaluate: to evaluate the quality services performed and to improve the quality of the services provided.

6. The Association takes measures: in accordance with its activity it takes measures to improve the situation in the administrative areas. 2. KSA structure (only a few important segments)

7."Association" has neither executive nor legislative powers (does not issue laws or executive body), does not contradict the constitution with article 4 and points 1-7 of this article.

8.ASK, issues decisions applicable to its members.

• The chairman of the association represents in the country and abroad for the mentioned common fields and competences (logical interpretation).

9.. The establishment of the "civil service" shall be in accordance with the Constitution with Article 101 - replaced with the title "Secretariat".

10. Establishment of joint-venture enterprises: in accordance with the constitution and the law on inter-municipal cooperation.

11. ASK relations with central authorities

KAS (item 11 of the agreement) may represent the interests of the municipality in the Constitutional Court in accordance with Article 112, point 4 of the Constitution (municipalities may challenge the constitutionality of laws or acts of the Government that violate the municipal's responsibilities or reduce municipal revenues in if the municipality is affected by that law or act.

Conclusion: The name "Association of Serb Municipalities" is not in accordance with Article 124 (Organization and Functioning of Local Self-Government) and is not in compliance with Article 16 (the supremacy of the Constitution, the name of the agreement contradict Article 81, point 1 , 2,3,4,5,, 6,7,8 (Legislation of vital interest), this designation does not comply with the standards of this Constitution. Kosovo Constitution based on Article 81 has defined the part of vital laws for which cannot be subject to a referendum. This implies, based on the logical, free and connected and evolutionary and systematic interpretation that: the name "Association of Serb Municipalities" is not in accordance with the constitution, municipalities based on Article 124 of the Constitution have no reference ethnic.

Additional clarification: The Constitution under Article 124 abrogates the right of municipalities to formulate such designations for the implementation of the law on local self-government and the law on inter-municipal cooperation through such designation.

Proposal: This association should be named: Agreement for Cooperation between Municipalities ...... based on Article 124.4 of the Constitution. II.

The denomination in accordance with the constitution is suggested: "Inter-Municipal Cooperation". The following are the names of municipalities....

1. The agreement is in accordance with Articles 58, 58 and 58.5 of the Constitution of Kosovo

Additional clarification: "Association Agreement" - does not conflict with the articles of the law on inter-communal cooperation, this law is in line with the Kosovo constitution and allows for inter-municipal cooperation including the establishment of joint public enterprises (section 9.1.4), as well as the establishment of a joint administrative body Article 9.1.2).

3. This Agreement does not contradict Article 22, paragraph 1 to 8 of the Constitution, either in Articles 53 and 59, points 1 to 14 of the Constitution.

4. The agreement is in accordance with article 7 of the constitutional (democratic values).

5. Based on Article 101, Paragraph 1 and 2, the Republic of Kosovo has a unique civil service and that only two levels of power have the right to recruit civil servants and finance this service.

CHAPTER THREE

1. Local Political Party

The term "local party" refers to all political forces that have internal organizational specs in the localities where they operate and who want to gain power through local elections or to gain governance in the locality where they operate, but apart from the parties, other civil society organizations have the right to run in elections to represent representatives of the representative body or to influence influence on decision-making in local government 1). Political capacities, respectively, the sixth spectrum of intellectual and socio-economic profiling of local parties are those where they consider that can run with the local government and be governed by them with the right efficiency and dedication. These parties have their branches and subordinates, have their own technical staff, fax, telephone, office, copier and social mobilizing factor, membership or support parties that have a better organization can have a positive impact on local government to gain positions in municipal bodies and to take responsibility for its people in the assembly. They need their actions to justify and, of course, the decisions they issue as a majority in the respective municipal assembly and so as to give clarification to the public for the decisions taken naturally hold responsibility for the functioning and transparency of the citizens. Political parties and other organizations are organized in such a way as to gather important information in the field and then articulate them to presenting the real circumstances on the ground 2) .Partitions that are more "big" with supporters and with many experts are more likely to exert greater influence than the party with small political capacities and fewer supporters. This multiple information gathered before the election campaign and after the campaign helps them to implement projects and their previously designed strategies, to make decisions and to implement them. Normal with realistic pragmatic decision-making opportunities. There are several segments of important considerations such as policy-making, institutional action powers and responsibilities under the law on local self-government or the juridical-political competencies of the highest organs given to the municipality as well as other important issues such as: pre-electoral campaigns, supporters, staff members, campaign organization and assistance at the national and parliamentary level of the country.

2. Civil Society

The theory of the influence of civil society in the exercise of state power derives from old thinkers such as Aristotle Hegel who, however depending on the organization, have and may have a great influence on the overall processes of the locality. Civil society is also composed of many volunteers with individual initiatives, group organizations that are independent of politics and the current party that governs local politics or presume to lead 4). Civil society can be powerful and may contain the economic group developed independently of parties but influential in economic circumstances. Civil society is also a significant number of NGOs in the municipalities. Civil society can create numerous ideas independent of the political party, can take independent free initiatives, with broader stakeholder interests or often have an impact on wide associations in society. Various affiliates also have a large group of volunteer people, their members who are active in civilian life in municipalities. Civil society also makes efforts to exercise direct influence if they can be members of municipal authorities or may exert influence outside the assembly as in politics, decision-making, accountability and development of local democracy 5). It is important not to suppress civil society but to be allowed and assisted in it different forms from parties to participate in decision-making. Civil society and their officials and also influence the increase of pressure on local parties that have an impact on policy making and decision-making. Civil society can affect the utilization of the municipal budget in the social economic developments in the municipalities. But another important segment is how many NGOs or other groups the other local unions can operate in localities. They can affect the improvement of civil services provided to citizens in the municipalities 6). Civil society can exercise "monitoring" of political actions and municipal decisions, then of policy making and in the implementation of promised policies during the campaigns. Civil society has ideas as well as its own proposals that directly influence the local government through as well as organizing numerous debates with citizens and other institutions.

3. Local Media

Local media are mitigating factors that affect the exercise of "pressure" in the sense of democratic control of meeting the interests of citizens and their demands arising from municipal life. The concept of local media - is to inform citizens about the different activities or events of institutional life, then political parties - opposition parties and civil society who tend to cover their activity in informing citizens rightfully. Media have an impact on all segments such as decision-making, policy-making, and global economic development. The media inform about the participation of citizens in local elections, the role of civil society, the global interest of citizens on policies proposed by the political party. Mostly, their activity is done through direct questions to the municipal, civil society authorities. is done through public media, local newspapers and then through electronic and visual media. Media diversity is very important to the locality where they operate independently and are not directly influenced by daily politics. But it should not be forgotten that in the local media life there are also press and political media dependent and influenced by the party. NGOs produce leaflets in localities where they operate in some situations that are evaluated as a process of informing citizens differently. It is important that local media should cover the general activity of the locality.

4. Local political culture - the involvement of citizens in the political life of the locality

Citizens' participation is related to what they are trying to present their remarks on public affairs of general interest. This does not only imply their participation in elections, electoral campaign of parties, petition writing, the organization of demonstrations, and participation of their participation in political party rallies. Citizen participation in elections is important for the development of democracy and the only democratic condition for social progress. Their participation in various activities implies the expression of their convictions, the pressure they exert on political leaders and society civilians and the media, and directly affect the trust of the local government in the actions it undertakes. The promotion of political trust by citizens, participation in elections, giving of different opinions, they give and direct and indirectly show their interests, dissatisfied Citizen's interest is greater in cases where promises are not realized and between the period of organizing local

43

elections when promising the parties during the campaign .Organizations are often obliged to hear the voice of the citizens about their decisions through local referendums on municipal issues where there is disagreement and petitions from citizens.

5, Civic Political Culture

Civic political culture is shown through various forms that show the "pleasure" or "disrespect" of local government ways of party or coalition parties. They carefully watch parties, the vocabulary of political personalities, the events in municipal assemblies, the decisions that emerge and "oversee" the parties 'ideas "whether or not to vote in the future. Citizens' participation in political or ideological decision making does not there is lack of support to the parties. Citizens are interested in the rate of taxation affecting their lives, global economic-social development, communal services, are they functional or not? Reactions are manifested according to actions occurring in municipal assemblies. "Agree" or "disagree" for the actions being done. Their demands may follow with the actions of manifesting global disputes in the Communes. They also have their own opinion to evaluate and respond to requests.

Through the implementation of legal norms, sub-legal acts issued by the municipality. Often, they through civic initiatives and group organization may seek political tolerance in the assemble, good will of the local government for tolerance within the political debates within the assembles, political flexibility in action, their credibility. Responses to citizens are more or less "dispersed" due to the different localities in the neighborhoods, villages where they live, and alleyways. The municipalities also have their own local maps. Citizens follow the implementation of the local government's political program and assembly decisions in facilitating their lives in municipalities.

6.Local Democracy

Local Democracy depends on many different municipal, socio-economic, political, electoral or electoral systems that are applicable to the election of representatives to municipal bodies, and depends on the territorial size of the municipality, the number of inhabitants, the geographic position of municipalities, their local boundaries, local status (competencies) of local governments such as villages, cities, central parts of the city, districts within the cities, heterogeneity of the local population, social, ethnic, religious, social development. important as well as various civic data for the commune, administrative data etc

7. Center Impacts in Locations

Such relocations should be observed in these segments:

Legal decentralization, fiscal decentralization, financial responsibility and legal administrative responsibility in matters of implementation of sub-legal acts. The administration implies the administrative capacities of the local government municipality, local staff and their functioning, the employed administrative officers and the political capacities that guide them. The role of administration is important and functionalized in various administrative activities that are in the service of citizens. In this case, the following elements are important: Quality of administrative staff, number of employees in the administration, the mechanism of responsibility to local government, and the distributive power within the administration.

8. The Impact of Local Government Policy:

-The decision-making process, decision-making, accountability and democratic performance of local government are important components for citizens.

8.1. Local Representatives

Ethnic, religious and political representatives of citizens, their social characteristics and their economic background, their political experience, their civic culture, the stability of their representation, their political composition and their engagement bodies or committees, the fragments, the majority representative, and minority impersonators.

8.2. Local economic and social development

It is important to distinguish these segments:

Economic developments or increase of production in the private and public sector at the municipal level then the development of transport, social infrastructure, annual commune annual income, increase of the number of inhabitants, village immigration and periodic reports of economic growth, number of births and the dead within the year, the percentage of citizens' education.

8.3.Local elections

Local elections are also very important for the functioning of democratic institutions through elections. The winning party or party that has won a certain majority of the electorate forms the eagle government. Depending on what is the percentage of the winning party constitutes the local government. Local elections involve the representation of citizens in municipal assemblies. Depending on the electoral system, the winning or coalition party forms the direct-line directives that directly engage in solving the problems of the citizens.

9. Municipal Assembly

Citizens choose their municipal representatives who further engage in improving the lives of citizens depending on the electoral system practiced by that proportional or majority system. Kosovo has so far practiced elections with the proportional system. The Assembly operates under the Statute. Kosovo under UN administration has issued the Regulation on the functioning of local government. The last regulation of 2007/30 precludes the functioning of municipal bodies. Municipalities have their municipal statutes issued and approved by municipal assemblies.

9.1. Local Government

In Kosovo for the first time the mayoral elections have been developed directly by the citizens of Kosovo with an open list of the proportional system that gives the right to the party or parties that have won votes in the formation of the local government through the allocation of the directors who received Directly to municipal life and are executives.

Local Government in Kosovo and needs in the transitional period

1. The local government reform,

2 Monitoring, Coordination and Support of Kosovo Municipalities,

3. Continuous work on capacity building of the MLGA administration and Kosovo Municipalities,

4. Coordination of activities in the implementation of international standards,

2. Effective MEF management of the human resources, technical and administrative resources of the MLGA. The MAPL is at the stage of the transitional developments of the continuous consolidation of work and through established Council of Europe's working groups and international experience and regional and European experiences made efforts find ways and modalities to derive the necessary laws and ongoing reform in the local area. One issue that was the reason for the reception was the issue of decentralization as long as this process does not end and is now considered closed. But there is only a phase of implementation, it is the case to work more and more efficiently to make the laws or complete the infrastructure currently existing except for the Law on the Functioning of the Prishtinë / Pristina Capital and some other pertinent acts related to power but there are other challenges that await institutional development at the local and central level. The issue of ongoing reform occurs in all countries like Spain, Germany and other France.

10.Reform

Political process: The political process related to the process of local government reform will continue in the coming years and requires coordination at two levels: on the one hand, the process involving the preparation and adoption of legislative infrastructure, which requires close co-operation with the municipalities, The Kosovo Assembly and political parties, community representatives and civil society. In parallel, the status talks are set to focus on aspects of Local Government Reform / Decentralization, including municipal competencies and territorial organization of Kosovo. For this, it is necessary to provide data and expertise from MLGA and coordination within MLGA, and certain groups for the development of status talks that are now concluded between Kosovo and Serbia should be provided. Kosovo is an independent state and that the commitment made earlier to implement reforms in the local government will be achieved step by step under international oversight by the EU and the US.

. Comparative analysis and comparative studies on a developed concept of local government in Kosovo: All existing and potential proposals that will follow, including the ideas of local, regional and international actors, are analyzed in detail by the political and technical experts within MLGA / Government 17). A team is set to be assisted by ad hoc established groups to analyze, collect and compare such proposals with existing international models and elaborate concepts (alternatives), and will formulate short-term recommendations to the Ministry / Government. In addition, the MLGA will sign a Memorandum of Understanding with neighboring ministries of neighboring countries (Macedonia, and in particular Albania) in order to ensure that these models, practices and lessons learned from the region are incorporated into Kosovo's plans for decentralization.

c. Transfer of competencies: MLGA has issued recommendations for transfer of competencies at the local level. From the relevant central institutions (Ministry of Agriculture, Ministry of Environment and Spatial Planning, Ministry of Education, Ministry of Trade and Industry, Ministry of Economy and Finance, UNMIK Pillar IV, KTA) immediate cooperation is required. The recommendations issued by the WG are approved by the Minister, and will then be incorporated into the Law on Local Self-Government. Then, after the approval of the LLNG, the GP will elaborate, in coordination with the municipalities, an implementation plan for the transfer of competencies selected in each municipality, and will monitor, monitor and evaluate the achieved results. The complete transfer of all new competencies will be achieved after the entry into force of the Law on Local Self-Government, which is expected to be issued by the Assembly of Kosovo.

d. Law on Local Self-Government: The Law on Local Self-Government is a key legislative priority for local government development. The law is quite detailed and includes the restriction of the legal status of municipalities, municipal financial competencies, the organization and functioning of municipal bodies, The city of Pristina will be governed by a new law on the capital, the law leaves open the opportunity to eventually give status to other cities of Kosovo such as cultural, other tourists. Municipalities, ACAs, NGOs and civil society were also invited to help draft this law, and then submitted to Parliament and approved. The law is under implementation and still needs to be well analyzed especially around this implementation process. 18). Now I have the approval of the law by the Assembly of the Republic of Kosovo.

e. Local Finance Law: The existing concept document that presents an analysis of existing deficiencies and recommendations for solving these shortcomings will be reviewed by a subgroup (technical) established for this purpose and then submitted to the Group Working for Local Finance. The Local Finance Working Group will compile a list of all existing laws pertaining to Municipal Finances, as well as existing models of the region and international ones. This concept may be required to be included in the Government's agenda for information or to receive their opinion on the new Law on Local Finance or the amendment of existing laws. The Law on Local Finances is compiled by the Law on Local Self-Government, and is sent to the Government for approval after it has been approved. The Law on Local

Self-Government (by the Parliament) in order to ensure that the Law on Local Finances will include all provisions contained in the Law on Local Self Government, in particular with regard to the competencies to be financed by the municipalities. Theoretically, this law is foreseen to be submitted to Government.

f. Law on Local Elections: The Electoral Forum should complete its work with clear recommendations for a future local election system before the end of 2005. But the legal draft has not yet been completed has already begun and needs to be harmonized, and therefore a mixed group should be established. A political agreement should be reached if this legislative act is to be considered a law adopted by the Kosovo Assembly, or UNMIK Regulation, with definitive preference for the first alternative 20). This legal act has to be issued six months before the local elections, which has not been issued until now. Local and central elections were held in November 2007. MLGA recommended holding regular local elections taking into account the existing 30 municipalities and the Pilot Municipal Units, which up until then could become a municipality, as well as the appointment of new local elections in 2008 after the completion of the Local Government Reform and in the territorial reorganization (implemented by that time), including the refreshing vote list.

Pilot projects: As far as the three Pilot Municipal Units are established and now functional, as a further step in their implementation is the drafting and approval of statutes and procedural rules that need to be elaborated and approved, the time for transfer of competencies is elaborated and premises and staff will be provided. The whole process should be monitored, monitored and eventually evaluated 22). Monitoring and evaluation should be based on the individual progress of pilot projects, focusing in particular on the following criteria: implementation of Kosovo's laws; capacity for service provision; economic sustainability and services provided to citizens. Monitoring and composition of the monitoring team should still be defined. The Government will inform the Assembly of the progress and progress achieved throughout the process and present the final evaluations for each Pilot Project at the end of the pilot period (before the local elections 2006). This assessment will serve as a basis for the decision to transform the Pilot Municipal Unit into the municipality after consideration and

k. approval by the Assembly. Regarding two Pilot Projects foreseen by the Serbian majority (Gračanica and Partesh), the government continues to open the Kosovo Serb bid and is ready to re-engage in talks on the launch of these two Pilot

Projects, based on the cooperation agreement close to the community and local representatives when they are willing and willing.

l. Capacity Building: Efforts to increase the capacity of the Pilot Municipal Units should continue and be specifically included in capacity building for civil servants of Pilot Municipal Units. KIPA has undertaken an assessment of the needs for capacity building of civil servants in municipalities and donor-funded capacity building projects in municipalities. For this, a report will be prepared with recommendations for further action as well as a list of necessary capacity building projects that will be submitted to donors.

m. Population Census: Population data is an absolute condition for territorial reorganization. The population census will be held in the following years as foreseen and should not be postponed. Any delay will lead to delays in the timetable related to the implementation of the decentralization process. Proper funding needs to be provided. The Ministry of Public Administration has initiated actions for civil registration of the population, where it will be supported by other institutions, as well as international ones regarding the monitoring of the census, so it was said earlier. MLGA and other institutions will provide its MAP assistance in whatever mode is required.

CHAPTER FOUR

President Ahtisaari's document

1.DECENRALIZATION

An advanced and sustainable system of local self-government in Kosovo will be established to address the concerns of Kosovo Serbs and other communities that do not constitute the majority in Kosovo and their members, to encourage and assure active participation in public life and to empowering good governance and the efficiency and effectiveness of Kosovo's public services in accordance with the following principles and provisions.

1.1 Basic Provisions

1.2 The local self-government in Kosovo will be based on the principles of the European Charter on Local Self-Government and in particular on the principle of subsidiarity.

1.3 Local Self-Government in Kosovo shall protect and promote internationally recognized human rights standards, with special regard to the needs of non-majority communities and their members in Kosovo.

1.4 The main principles of decentralization shall be laid down in the Constitution as set out in Article 8 of the Annex to this Agreement.

2. Kosovo Legislation on Local Governance

Kosovo shall issue the law on local government within 120 days of the entry into force of this Agreement, which shall strengthen the capitals and organization of the municipalities as provided for in this Annex and in Annex XII 27). Kosovo shall issue a new Law on Municipal boundaries within 120 days of the entry into force of this Agreement, which will define the new municipalities as provided in this Annex and in Annex XII 28). Kosovo shall issue the basic legislation in accordance with the principles set out in this Annex , in order to ensure impartial treatment and minimum standards for all municipalities, regarding the regulation and management of public affairs falling into their responsibilities, particularly respecting the principle of subsidiarity.

3. Municipalities Competencies

Municipalities in Kosovo will have full and exclusive competences, however, regarding the local interest, respecting the standards set out in the legislation in force according to this document:

In the following areas (further, own constraints).

a. Local economic development.

b Urban and local planning.

c. land use and development:

d. Implementation of building regulations and building control standards

e. Local Environmental Protection.

f. Provision and maintenance of public services and utilities, including water supply, drainage and drainage, sewage treatment, waste management, local roads, local transport and local heating schemes.

g. Responding to local emergency situations.

h. Provision of pre-primary, primary and secondary public education, including registration and licensing of education institutions, employment, payment of salaries and training of instructors and education administrators.

i. Provision of primary public health care.

j Family and other services.

Public b.

l Public Praise.

m Licensing local services and facilities, including those related to entertainment, cultural and leisure activities, food, housing, markets, street vendors, local public transport and taxis.

n. Development of roads, neighborhoods and other public places.

o. Provision and maintenance of public parks and spaces tourism.

q Cultural and leisure activities.

Any other matter that is expressly not excluded from their competences or that is not assigned to another authority.

4.. Extended Municipal Self Improvement Competencies

Certain designated municipalities in Kosovo will have their own enhanced competencies as follows:

The municipality of Mitrovica in the North will have this competency for higher education, including registration and licensing of education, employment, salary and training instructors and education administrators. Mitrovica North, Gracanica and Shtërpcë municipalities will have competences for provision of secondary healthcare, including registration and licensing of healthcare institutions, employment, salaries and training of health care personnel and administrators.

All municipalities in which the Serb community is a majority shall have the authority to exercise responsibility for cultural affairs, including, in accordance with the constituencies of Annex V to this Agreement, the protection and promotion of cultural heritage of Serbs and others within the municipal territory such as and support for the local religious community.

Advanced Rights of Participants in Election and Discharge of Police Station Commanders. As to these extended self-governing competencies, Kosovo will issue framework legislation to provide equal access to public services, minimum qualitative and quantitative standards in service delivery public: minimum qualifications of staff and training facilities, general principles on licensing and accreditation of public service providers.

5.Administrative review of municipal activities

Ahtisaari's document mentions the review of municipal activities by central authorities in the areas of their own competences will be limited to ensuring compliance with the Kosovo Constitution and applicable laws. The Administrative Supervisory Authority may require the Commission to resubmit decisions or other legal acts deemed to be incompatible with the Constitution or the laws adopted pursuant to this Agreement. The request shall not suspend the execution of a municipal decision or any other legal act. The municipality accepts the request in accordance with Article 6.1.1 of this Annex, it may decide to suspend the execution of a decision or other legal act pending review by the municipal authorities. If the Municipality refuses the Referral or verifies its decision or under review, the administrative supervisory authority may challenge the decision or other legal act in the district court competent for the territory of the municipality. The District Court may order, as an interim measure, the suspension of the enforcement of the contested decision or other legal act.

Regarding municipal delegated powers, central authorities may consider the appropriateness of the draft law or other act adopted by the municipality, in addition to its compliance with the Kosovo Constitution and the legislation adopted in accordance with this agreement and thereafter, may suspend, modify or replace, where appropriate, the execution of the site.

5.1. Education:

Regarding the curriculum of Kosovo schools teaching in the Serbian language, schools that can learn in their mother tongue can use Serbian government curricula or textbooks and with notice of the Kosovo government, respectively MEST, in cases that the Government of Kosovo has remarks and then according to this document will be formed an independent commission to review Kosovo's compliance with the Kosovo Constitution. This commission will be a mix of 3 Kosovo Assembly deputies who are Serbian representative and three representatives from the Ministry of Education (MEST) and a member representing the International Civilian Mission in Kosovo. Ahtisaari's paper also speaks for the University of Mitrovica, which according to him is the autonomous institute of higher education, it will adopt its Statute, will determine the organization and its internal governance as well as procedures and interaction with public authorities in accordance with the central framework legislation to be reviewed by an independent commission. Municipality - North Mitrovica will have the right to nominate two members of the University Board. Mitrovica municipality of the north is still said to cooperate with any other municipality.

5.2. Public finances

Municipalities will form their own budgets covering tasks that fall within their competences. Central Legislation will determine the public management and financial responsibility requirements applicable to all municipalities in accordance with international standards. Municipalities will collect taxes, fees and payments. Grants from central conditional funds will take into account the allocation and spending of central funds. Grant allocation will take into account the adequate allocation of resources of non-majority communities to the respective municipalities, a system of equilibrium and reasonable stability in municipal revenues will be set through law in accordance with international standards 33).

6. Inter-communal Cooperation

This cooperation is based on the principles of the European Charter for Local Self-Government; municipalities will cooperate and establish municipal partnerships with other municipalities for mutual interest. The municipal community can undertake all necessary actions for implementing and exercising functional cooperation through, inter alia, the establishment of a decision-making body composed of representatives appointed by the parliamentary committees of the communes, employment and dismissal of administrative staff and advisers and decisions on funding needs and other operational partnership needs. These inter-partnership activities and decisions that will be issued to be reported to the center .Communities according to the European Charter can form associations or participate in Kosovo municipal associations. Ahtisaari's plan also speaks for cooperation with Serb municipalities in Serbia as well as financing and granting of other grants from Serbian government to Serbian municipalities, they will be transparent and funds will be sent to Kosovo commercial bank account.

7. Establishment of new municipalities

The new municipalities will be established and will be determined by the new Law on Municipal Borders. After the entry into force of this Law, the International Civilian Representative will undertake all the necessary preparations to ensure that until the moment of holding local elections, separate and establish all sources of revenue, properties and administrative structures required for the establishment and operation of new municipalities. The NPC will appoint according to this plan the new preparatory municipal teams (MPTs) to prepare for the establishment of communes new relevant and other related tasks are required by the ICR. During such preparations, the executive functions with respect to the new municipalities and the provision of public services for them will remain the responsibility of the former municipalities in the council with the MPT. Immediately after the local elections are over, all executive functions and powers will be transferred from prior municipalities to newly elected municipalities of new municipalities in accordance with this Agreement.

Kosovo will engage in consultations with non-majority communities, where this community constitutes at least 75% of the residents in a settlement where they comprise at least 5000 people in order to establish new municipalities.

8. Mitrovica and Ahtisaari Plan

Two new municipalities in Mitrovica and North and South will be established in Mitrovica. The joint board of North and South municipalities will be established to develop functional co-operation in the areas of their competences under the joint venture agreement. The joint bill will consist of 11 members, with five representatives elected from each municipality and one international representative to be elected by the PCN.PCN will open an office in Mitrovica that will function as law and order, free movement, return of displaced persons, property rights, housing, economic development. In the 120-day period, the SRSG will establish temporary communal structures in coordination with the ICR for the new Mitrovicë / Mitrovica municipality. Under the ceilings set out in the Annex to the Annex. After the transition period, these temporary communal structures will remain under the authority of the PCN until the first local elections in this municipality.

9. Population census and review of decentralization provisions

One year after the implementation of this document from Kosovo with the ICR with counseling will make the population census in accordance with international standards and will be subject to international observation. An international agency, in accordance with neighboring countries, shall register refugees and displaced persons who wish to return to Kosovo. This document provides further information on the provisions of this Annex on the establishment of new municipalities, including their administrative boundaries, revised and amended as necessary by the ICR, in close coordination with the Government of Kosovo and the Community Consultative Council, within six months from the submission of final results of the census .

CAPTER FIVE

1. Vision

The local government of Kosovo is responsible for providing all the public services that belong to it under the European Charter for Local Self-Government, while at the same time building the capacity of governance and human resources and developing e-governance to enable these services to provide efficiently and qualitatively. Each Kosovo municipality has a favorable investment environment, which enables a sustainable local economic development.

1.1. Definition and description of key objectives

Internal organization

Implementation and Stabilization of Local Governance Reform and its full functioning by 2013 based on the Government Framework Reform Program document and outcomes from the Kosovo status talks. This involves the transfer of competencies from the central level of all responsibilities based on the European Charter for Local Self-Government.

Municipalities create conditions for increasing the level of budget independence on a general average to 35% (this is a variable percentage depending on municipalities, because some municipalities have greater resources and opportunities, currently 20.4%) by extending the range of of own source revenues and increasing the collection rate by 70% by 2013. Municipal capacity to create own budgets, especially new municipalities and municipalities with a level below the municipal development average, should be taken into account.

Improve the quality of work and efficiency in local administration in all areas of services that are in the mandate of municipalities in order to provide the most quality services to citizens by 2013.

1.2. Infrastructure for economic and social development

Each municipality must have drafted or adapted the local economic development strategy according to the unique methodology of this planning, based on the Kosovo Strategy and Development Plan, no later than 12 months after its approval. By the end of 2007 all municipalities should draft plans for regulating the territory of the municipality (development plan, urban development plan and urban regulatory plan) based on the Law on Spatial Planning. Until 2008, industrial zones are regulated in all municipalities. By 2013, increase the number of joint projects from inter-municipal cooperation (municipalities within Kosovo) in order to increase the quality and efficiency of municipal administration and infrastructure services and reduce the cost. Until 2013, all municipalities will be twinned with at least one municipality of another country.

2. Public Services

By 2013, 90% of the population in urban areas and 70% in rural areas consume controlled water. The entire urban area with sewage systems will pour and store the sewage and atmospheric waters outside the territory, while 70% of the rural settlements wastewater will be deposited out of the inhabited territory.

3. Definition and description of key policies

Drafting organic laws in line with local government reform. The constitution of the Municipal Assemblies and the election of political leaders should be done, the constitution of all mandated bodies of the Municipal Assemblies.

Establish the Steering Boards for the functioning of public utilities that manage municipal infrastructure services. Reorganize directorates and relations and regulate the work and responsibilities of the Municipal Steering Board.

MLGA to establish unique governance criteria and define organizational levels for the purpose of functionalizing the administration in general, and increasing efficiency and professionalism.

• Central level policy: Creating a system of proportional grants allocation.

• Local level policy: Creating a system for increasing own source revenues.

• Establish mechanisms for monitoring and evaluating the performance of municipalities.

• Creation of mechanisms in order to increase the quality and efficiency of municipal services for citizens.

• Standardization of methodologies for drafting strategies for local economic development.

• Drafting plans for regulating the territory of municipalities based on the law on spatial planning.

• Promote policies on forms of inter-municipal cooperation.

• Promoting policies on forms of inter-municipal external cooperation.

• Creating mechanisms so that municipal public utilities manage all waterworks built in rural areas.

4.Kosovo : Action Plan :Strategic objectives 2016-2026

Sustainable local economic development:

1. Draft policies on local economic development;

2. Draft policies on the management of public property;

3. Draft policies on regional development

Creation of development policies:

1.Improve the legal framework and change the municipal finance system;

2. Strengthen the financial and economic management capacity of local municipal officials;

3. Support businesses and farmers in expansion of their activities at the national and international level;

4. Increase capacities of municipalities for the management of natural resources in order to create social and economic matter.

5. Construction of road infrastructure stainability at the local level:

Construction of local roads; 2. Construction of rural roads; 3. Naming and marking of local roads :

5. Preparing young people to join the workforce

1. Establish vocational schools

2. Open/functionalize innovation centers;

3. Develop special training programs;

4. Establish low rate credit schemes;

5. Develop programming schemes for employment in the agricultural sector

6. Support to businesses and agriculture:

1. Conduct a survey on the possibilities of increasing the agricultural production and business development;

2. Develop grant schemes to support businesses and the agricultural sector;

3. Establish mechanisms to stimulate local businesses and products;

4. Support young people and women in business through their lending activities; 5. Support municipalities in promoting businesses and products in fairs organized inside and outside the municipality.

7.Revision and creation of the legal base:

1.Evaluate and harmonize the national legislation;

2. Harmonize the legislation with the Acquis Communautaire.

3. Harmonize the secondary legislation with national legislation and Acquis Communautaire.

4. Clarify and horizontally scale the powers of municipalities based on their potential and capacity.

5. Establish full legal and administrative mechanisms for an effective supervision of the legality in the municipal work.

8.Increase the efficiency at the local administration:

1.Build institutional capacities of municipalities;

2. Enhance the representative role of municipal bodies;

3. Create the service for legal advices to citizens;

4. Build professional capacities of municipalities;

5. Build physical and technical capacities of municipalities;

6. Identify services that can be offered online;

7. Organize and develop institutional memory in order to support the work of administration.

9. The effective participation of citizens in governance:

1.Develop policies encouraging the participation of citizens in the decision making;
2. Develop policies encouraging youth centers in villages;

3. Develop policies encouraging village councils;

4. Develop policies for the inclusion and involvement of pensioners in the public life;

5. Develop policies on engagement of persons with disabilities;

6. Develop policies to encourage participation of women and social categories of non-protected;

7. Develop local policies for the treatment of street children;

8. Develop local policies for creation of social, economic, youth, sports and culture networks.

10.Development of professional capacities:

1.Create legal mechanisms for the establishment of the Academy on Local Self-Government;

2. Establish the "Academy on Local Self-Government";

3. Establish administrative and professional mechanisms for professional capacity building;

4. Build professional capacities of local institutions.

11.Building managerial capacities of the administration:

1. Ensure the legal basis for the mandatory participation of municipal officials in trainings;

2. Develop integrated training programs in the field of public administration and good governance for the development of professional capacity of municipalities;

3. Build capacity for planning and implementation of work plans and projects;

4. Clarify the mechanisms of supervision, internal audit and reporting;

5. Increase the organizational culture and behavior of municipal employees with stakeholders;

6. Professional assessment of achievement at work.

12.The involvement of civil society and the private sector in the service delivery:

1. Develop institutional mechanisms for involvement of civil society in the service delivery;

2. Develop joint public-private projects.

Supervision and control:

Build capacities to supervise and control the implementation of projects and services.

13.Increase democratic values through involvement of citizens

1. Develop policies for democratic involvement of citizens in the joint work;

2. Draft program for joint engagement with citizens.

Development of a sense of volunteerism among citizens

1. Develop information and training programs for the cultivation of a sense of volunteerism;

14. Establishment of centers for voluntary work

 Draft plans for citizens' involvement in the voluntary work within the urban and rural neighborhoods;

15. Strengthening of civil society and new businesses:

1. Involve citizens through participation in the planning process;

2. Draft municipal plans for stimulation of young entrepreneurs;

 3. Develop educational and training programs for secondary school students;

 4. Establish policies aimed at creating a sustainable environment for businesses and small & medium enterprises;

5. Engage experienced business community in mentoring programs for young entrepreneur.

16. Promotion of cultural and natural heritage

1. Develop policies for the development and protection of municipal heritage;

 2. Improve operational capacity for the management of the resources of the local heritage and increase the participation of communities and local institutions;

 3. Demonstrate effective planning and management of local resources through active community participation in the processes of municipal and regional development plans;

 4. Strengthen the operational capacity intergovernmental and civil society mechanisms for an effective communication between the central and local level;

5. Increase the awareness for the values of municipal heritage through active involvement of local authorities and communities.

17. Promotion of ethnic and linguistic diversity

1. Draft local plans on ethnic and linguistic diversity;

2. Promote values of ethnic diversity and equality of language use;

3. Demonstrate the promotion of gender equality and social inclusion of vulnerable groups in the development processes at the local level;

Local self-governance is a crucial element in bringing political representatives closer to their constituencies and forging strong links between citizens and public institutions. This connection makes it possible for officials to understand the problems and concerns of local communities, design policy solutions that maximize social wellbeing and provide services that respond to citizens' needs[54]. Functioning of local self-governments is thus a good indicator of the commitment of political representatives to serve the public interest. In the regional comparison of local self-governments, Kosovo comes close to the bottom with 26.7% of criteria met[55]. The last Albania scores a mere 12.1% while the most successful Montenegro fulfills 57.5% of them. Two macro-level conclusions can be drawn from these results: local self-governance is of varying quality in the Western Balkans (in terms of accessibility, awareness, integrity and transparency of information) and it is generally lower than for other institutions. This suggests that strengthening democracy and service delivery in the region will require special attention to local self-governance. Kosovo's overall score is negatively affected by lower levels of accessibility and integrity, although the difference between the worst and best performing variables, accessibility and awareness, is less than 5%. All four examined areas should therefore be targeted by policy-makers working to improve local self-governance in Kosovo[56]. This seems all the more so urgent as the local self-governments come out of the evaluation as the second least successful institution within Kosovo, only executive agencies fare worse with less than one fifth of indicators fulfilled (19.6%).

The municipalities subject to the assessment are Dragash, Ferizaj, Gllogoc, Gračanica, Klina, Kllokot, Malishevo, Mamusha, Mitrovica, Partesh, Podujevë/Podujevo, Ranilug, Štrpse, Zubin Potok, Zvečan. The most successful of them are Mitrovica (59.8%), Dragash (44.5%) and Podujevo (39.7%), with Ferizaj and Malishevo trailing closely behind. At the tail's end can be found Zvečan, Zubin Potok and Partesh who meet a mere 0% to 1% of benchmarks. It should be noted that this is mainly due to the slow process of establishment of new municipalities

---

[54] Group of authors Analysis of openness of local self-government in Kosovo, pp4
[55] Group of Authors:Analysis of openness of local self-government in Kosovo pp 4
[56] Groups of Authors: Analysis of openness of local self-government in Kosovo pp5,2017

63

in Northern Kosovo most of which are operational to a very limited extent (Mayors and their cabinets)[57].

18. Integrity Meeting

Integrity Meeting: the benchmarks for integrity in local self-governance seems to pose difficulties to most municipal institutions across the region. Only Montenegro achieves a higher score in this domain (71.4%), the rest of the Western Balkan countries scoring 40% or lower[58]. Kosovo thus finds itself in the middle of the ranking with 25.5% of integrity criteria aimed at preventing conflict of interest met. Disaggregating at the municipal level uncovers uniformity across Kosovo's local governments: the only criterion fulfilled by all municipalities is the public availability of the asset cards of officials. All the other criteria, such as existence of public mechanisms for reporting of illegal practices, existence of anticorruption plans/procedures and concomitant implementing body of the latter, are unmet by all but two municipalities, Gllogoc and Mitrovica[59]. Nevertheless, even they do not fulfil all of them, scoring only 64.3%. Fighting corruption is a sensitive and complex issue at all levels of governance; it is therefore no surprise that it is the case in Kosovo municipalities too. However, contrasted with the nation-wide institutions, local governments have so far failed to institute mechanisms, plans and procedures needed for anti-corruption interventions. This should be a starting point for eliminating corruption at the municipal level .

Transparency Kosovo's local governments are among the least transparent when it comes to budget, organizational in formation and public procurement transparency. As in other areas, Kosovo (27.5%) is at the tail before Albania (9.5%) and falling behind Montenegro in the lead with 58%. The most successful municipalities in terms of budget transparency are Dragash and Podujevo, although they meet just about half of the benchmarks in this category. On the other end of the spectrum are Mamusha, Partesh, Zubin Potok and Zvečan who do not fulfil a single criterion. The areas found the most problematic by many local governments are publication of information concerning the municipal debt, conduct of consultations on draft budget and publishing results of such consultations, timely submission of budgets to Assemblies, and pu blication of the Citizens Budget. The lack of budgetary transparency should be addressed by

---

[57] Groups of Authors, Analysis of openness of local self-government in Kosovo,pp5 ,2017
[58] Groups of Authors: Analysis of openness of local self-government in Kosovo pp7,2017
[59] Groups of Authors: Analysis of openness of local self-government in Kosovo pp7,2017

municipalities as a matter of priority as transparent use of public financ e is an essential precondition for delivery of public services and trust between constituents and their representatives. Great diversity can be observed in Kosovo's municipalities in relation to the transparency of information on public procurement. While some fulfill few or no criteria (Gračanica, Kllokot, Mamusha, Partesh, Ranilug, Zubin Potok, Zvečan), others score high (Gllogoc) and even meet them all (Malisheva, Mitrovica, Podujeva). The indicators relate to publication of procurement plans, calls, decisions, contracts and annexes of local governments. The degree of organizational information transparency is slightly more uniform across municipalities, most scoring around 30%. Partesh, Zvečan, Zubin Potok are the outliers on the low end and Dragash (41.6%)[60] and Mitrovica (60.4%) stand out on the high end[61]. The most troublesome areas are publication of information on property, access to streaming of municipal assembly sessions, publication of detailed urban and spatial plans, shares of public enterprises, annual work plans, and personnel information on the website[62]. While addressing some of them would require technical and financial resources that might not be readily available to many municipalities (e.g. to offer direct streaming of assembly sessions), most can be implemented without extra financial burden and within reasonable timelines. This would help improve Kosovo's current ranking in local self-governance transparency.

Region A regional result of openness of local self-government is disappointing and amounts to only 34%.[63] Municipalities resemble black boxes more than key institutions of citizens' service[64]. All problems recorded in Montenegro provide a credible picture of situation at a local level in the region, where the situation is worse than in our country. The policy of openness must be a policy of all municipalities and find its place among other significant state policies. It is high time to start with solving this issue. Research methodology The openness is a key condition of democracy since it allows citizens to receive information and knowledge about an equal participation in a political life, effective decision-making and holding institutions responsible for policies they conduct. A number of

[60] Groups of Authors: Analysis of openness of local self-government in Kosovo pp8,2017
[61] Groups of Authors: Analysis of openness of local self-government in Kosovo pp8,2017
[62] Groups of Authors: Analysis of openness of local self-government in Kosovo pp8,2017
[63] Groups of Authors: Analysis of openness of local self-government in Kosovo pp11,2017

[64] Groups of Authors: Analysis of openness of local self-government in Kosovo pp11,2017

countries undertake specific actions towards increasing transparency and accountability of institutions. The Regional index of openness of local self-governments is developed in order to define to which extent citizens of the Western Balkans receive opportune and understandable information from their institutions[65]. The Regional index of openness measures to which extent institutions of the Western Balkans are open for citizens and society, based on the following four principles:

1. Transparency,

2. Accessibility

3. Integrity and

4. Awareness.

The principle of transparency includes that organizational information, budget and public procurement procedure are publicly available and published[66]. Accessibility is related to ensuring and respecting procedures for a free access to information, improving accessibility of information through a mechanism of public debates and strengthening interaction with citizens. Integrity includes mechanisms for the prevention of corruption[67]. The last principle, effectiveness, is related to monitoring and evaluation of policies which are conducted by institutions. Following the international standards, recommendations and examples of good practice, these principles are further developed through specific, quantitative and qualitative indicators, which are evaluated on the basis of: information accessibility on official websites of institutions, legal framework's quality for specific questions, other sources of public informing and questionnaires delivered to institutions[68]. The set of recommendations and guidelines, directed towards institutions, was developed on the basis of research results.

CHAPTER SIX

1. Refocusing on the Western Balkans local governance

---

[65] Groups of Authors: Analysis of openness of local self-government in Kosovo pp11,2017
[66] Groups of Authors: Analysis of openness of local self-government in Kosovo pp11,2017
[67] Groups of Authors: Analysis of openness of local self-government in Kosovo pp10,2017

[68] Groups of Authors: Analysis of openness of local self-government in Kosovo pp10,2017

The celebration of the 60th anniversary of the Treaties of Rome, establishing the European Economic Community and paving the way for what today is known as the EU since the Lisbon Treaty, is a good opportunity to direct the EU's attention to a neighboring region which seemed to have lost the priority on the EU agenda. The fact that the Western Balkans shared a post-war experience like the six signatory countries of the Rome Treaty and by taking into consideration the crucial role of the region for the preservation of peace throughout Europe, led the EU from 2000 until 2008 to launch activities to enhance stability, mutual understanding, peaceful coexistence and economic growth through trade embedded into a perspective of future EU integration[69]. Dynamics, reform willingness, enthusiasm, hope and motivation generated since then have been fading gradually and gave way to apathy, reform stalemate, impatience and rising skepticism regarding EU membership. At present tensions in the Western Balkans are rising. Social protests in the whole region are piling up reflecting the political and socio-economic standstill and increasing instability. These protests are met with mounting geopolitical pressure to destabilize the region and draw countries away from EU accession and NATO membership. In the light of these events, witnessed by EU foreign affairs Chief Federica Mogherini during her trip to several Western Balkan countries in March 2017, EU leaders have expressed alarm at the problems and reaffirmed their commitment to support stability and to deepen political and economic ties with and within the region. In fact, the EU Council Summit conclusions of 9 March 2017 refer to the situation in the Western Balkans as "fragile" stressing the importance of reforms, good neighborly relations and reaffirm its "unequivocal support for the European perspective of the Western Balkans". It was made clear that the EU remains committed and engaged at all levels to support the countries of the region in conducting EU oriented reforms and projects. In this context, the Network of Associations of Local Authorities of South-East Europe (NALAS) offers its institutional support and cooperation as an important stakeholder to work together with EU institutions in a Partnership for stability and growth to promote democratic reforms, good governance, the rule of law and sustainable development at local level in the Western Balkans[70]. NALAS

---

[69] Western Balkans in the loop, Local Governments and their Associations as key stakeholders in the EU Integration process, http: //www. bacid.eu /images/ 0/02/ Position_Paper_on_the_Western_Balkans_and_local_governments_in_the_EU_integration _%282%29.pdf pp1,2014
[70] Western Balkans in the loop, Local Governments and their Associations as key stakeholders in the EU Integration process, http: //www. bacid.eu /images/ 0/02/

has been committed since its creation in 2001 to the promotion of local democracy under the auspices of the Stability Pact and the Council of Europe, to contribute to the reconciliation and stabilization process in the region and henceforth subscribes to the process of the European integration of the whole region in a bottom-up approach.1 We strongly believe that change processes can only be sustainable and generate the desired impact if they are supported from the local level upwards by convinced, pro-active and committed citizens in a strategic alliance with public administration and authorities sharing the same vision[71]. Decentralization as a pillar of the democratic reform process is crucial for social cohesion, stability and peace in the Western Balkan countries and for the future of Europe. If Europe wants to be close to its future citizens, then it has to go local. The EU is about people, for people and around people[72]. The location where people live, act, meet and liaise directly with government and public administration is the local level! A functional bottom-up approach depends on an effective coordination and cooperation between local and central government level to be successful. The following proposals aim to strengthen dialogue facilities between the EU and the local level[73]. They are conceived as a contribution to adapt EU support instruments to better correspond to the needs of local authorities in preparing for EU accession and the adoption of standards by local public administrations. Furthermore, a brief analysis of the most pressing issues within the region should stress the importance

---

Position_Paper_on_the_Western_Balkans_and_local_governments_in_the_EU_integration _%282%29.pdf pp1,2014

[71] Western Balkans in the loop, Local Governments and their Associations as key stakeholders in the EU Integration process, http: //www. bacid.eu /images/ 0/02/ Position_Paper_on_the_Western_Balkans_and_local_governments_in_the_EU_integration _%282%29.pdf pp1,2014

[72] Western Balkans in the loop, Local Governments and their Associations as key stakeholders in the EU Integration process, http: //www. bacid.eu /images/ 0/02/ Position_Paper_on_the_Western_Balkans_and_local_governments_in_the_EU_integration _%282%29.pdf pp1,2014

Western Balkans in the loop, Local Governments and their Associations as key stakeholders in the EU Integration process, http: //www. bacid.eu /images/ 0/02/ Position_Paper_on_the_Western_Balkans_and_local_governments_in_the_EU_integration _%282%29.pdf pp1,2014

[73] Western Balkans in the loop, Local Governments and their Associations as key stakeholders in the EU Integration process, http: //www. bacid.eu /images/ 0/02/ Position_Paper_on_the_Western_Balkans_and_local_governments_in_the_EU_integration _%282%29.pdf pp1,2014

to conceive LGAs and LGs as crucial stakeholders and strategic partners in the EU integration and reform process in strengthening local democracy[74].

Proposals for dialogue facilitation EU institutions should bear in mind the specificities of local and regional authorities as one tier of government and engage with local authorities in multi-stakeholder dialogues on issues related to EU integration and reform processes[75]. It should be stressed that local and regional governments are both policy makers and service providers according to rights and obligations embedded in their national legislations. EU programming should recognize this fact by simplifying e.g. financial rules and allowing support to local government civil servant staff via its instruments and facilities honoring the principle of subsidiarity and acknowledging the importance of Associations of Local Authorities as stakeholder and interlocutor[76]. It is therefore necessary to implement a more inclusive consultation processes at all stages of planning, programming and decision-making on all issues affecting local government taking into account specific role, competences, tasks and responsibilities of local governments which are different from other local actors (i.e. private and civil sector) EU Commission - Technical or administrative unit for LGAs and LGs to address to One of the mayor impediments for LGAs and LGs are the restrictions they face addressing the EU Commission. They are not a stand-alone partner for DG NEAR, but communication and cooperation is realized with the central government. Today there is no technical or administrative unit in DG NEAR dealing separately with LGs in candidate countries. We strongly recommend to revert this

---

[74] Western Balkans in the loop, Local Governments and their Associations as key stakeholders in the EU Integration process, http: //www. bacid.eu /images/ 0/02/ Position_Paper_on_the_Western_Balkans_and_local_governments_in_the_EU_integration _%282%29.pdf pp1,2014
[75] Western Balkans in the loop, Local Governments and their Associations as key stakeholders in the EU Integration process, http: //www. bacid.eu /images/ 0/02/ Position_Paper_on_the_Western_Balkans_and_local_governments_in_the_EU_integration _%282%29.pdf pp2,2014
[76] Western Balkans in the loop, Local Governments and their Associations as key stakeholders in the EU Integration process, http: //www. bacid.eu /images/ 0/02/ Position_Paper_on_the_Western_Balkans_and_local_governments_in_the_EU_integration _%282%29.pdf pp2,2014

69

situation and to consider LGAs as a main stakeholder and interlocutor in the EU accession process[77].

European Parliament Working Group Working Groups are the backbone of the EP's political work. Here common positions and strategies on major policy areas are summoned and specific recommendations are submitted[78]. The former SEE working Group of the EP was an effective forum to address issues of common interest and played a major role in paving Croatia's accession to the EU. We recommend that the political parties represented in the EP and interested in EU relations with the Western Balkans consider the reestablishment of the former SEE Working Group or the set-up of a Western Balkans Working Group[79]. Western Balkans Cooperation Days the EP organizes every year special events focusing on specific geographical areas, like the Mediterranean. NALAS invites the EP to consider the organization of the Western Balkans Cooperation Days on an annual basis in cooperation with the Committee of the Regions[80]. Instrument for Pre-Accession - IPA II the Multi-Country Indicative Strategy (2014-2020) IPA II does not address local authorities as a key layer of governance. The lack of components designed for local development and the specific needs of cities, towns and local government entities bear witness of this omission[81]. Besides, for a majority of municipalities in the accession countries the perception prevails that EU

[77] Western Balkans in the loop, Local Governments and their Associations as key stakeholders in the EU Integration process, http: //www. bacid.eu /images/ 0/02/ Position_Paper_on_the_Western_Balkans_and_local_governments_in_the_EU_integration _%282%29.pdf pp2, 6.04.2014

[78] Western Balkans in the loop, Local Governments and their Associations as key stakeholders in the EU Integration process, http: //www. bacid.eu /images/ 0/02/ Position_Paper_on_the_Western_Balkans_and_local_governments_in_the_EU_integration _%282%29.pdf pp2, 6.04.2014
[79] Western Balkans in the loop, Local Governments and their Associations as key stakeholders in the EU Integration process, http: //www. bacid.eu /images/ 0/02/ Position_Paper_on_the_Western_Balkans_and_local_governments_in_the_EU_integration _%282%29.pdf pp2, 6.04.2014
[80] Western Balkans in the loop, Local Governments and their Associations as key stakeholders in the EU Integration process, http: //www. bacid.eu /images/ 0/02/ Position_Paper_on_the_Western_Balkans_and_local_governments_in_the_EU_integration _%282%29.pdf pp2, 6.04. 2014
[81] Western Balkans in the loop, Local Governments and their Associations as key stakeholders in the EU Integration process, http: //www. bacid.eu /images/ 0/02/ Position_Paper_on_the_Western_Balkans_and_local_governments_in_the_EU_integration _%282%29.pdf pp2,6.04. 2014

projects/programs are still too complex to be coped with given the circumstances within local administrations and the diversity of realities they represent[82]. The Commission's efforts/promises to simplify EU Fundraising via project/program access were largely counteracted by increasingly sophisticated and complex fund control mechanisms. A balance should be struck between feasible auditing/control mechanisms and the capacity on the spot at regional and local level to be able to put them into practice. NALAS invites the EU Commission to include LGAs to be part of the IPA negotiation, programming, monitoring and evaluation process[83]. This consideration should comprise the regional as well as the national consultation process. Civil Society Organization's – Local Authorities (CSO-LA) program The CSO-LA program managed by DG DEVCO as part of the Development Cooperation Instrument DCI, supports civil society organizations and local authorities as drivers of development. It enables beneficiaries to honor their ability to provide help and encourages long-term partnerships linking civil society and local authorities in order to play a bigger role in development strategies. The lack of access to the DCI CSO/LA program in the current period (2014-2020) is a big loss for Local Authorities of the IPA II beneficiary countries. Since there is no similar/comparable program available in IPA II, NALAS recommends the launch of a CSO-LA program for the region. Bridge Fund Facility for Local Self-Governments to pre-finance EU funded projects A main challenge municipalities face throughout the region is related to pre-financing of EU projects. For the implementation of projects in the frame of Cross-Border, Transnational Cooperation and most of other EU programs, local governments have to pre-finance in large part up to 90% of the funds[84]. This implies that pre-financing has to be covered by their own resources for project activities until they are refunded by the EU, which in some

---

[82] Western Balkans in the loop, Local Governments and their Associations as key stakeholders in the EU Integration process, http: //www. bacid.eu /images/ 0/02/ Position_Paper_on_the_Western_Balkans_and_local_governments_in_the_EU_integration _%282%29.pdf pp2,6.04.2014

[83] Western Balkans in the loop, Local Governments and their Associations as key stakeholders in the EU Integration process, http: //www. bacid.eu /images/ 0/02/ Position_Paper_on_the_Western_Balkans_and_local_governments_in_the_EU_integration _%282%29.pdf pp2,6.04.2014

[84] Western Balkans in the loop, Local Governments and their Associations as key stakeholders in the EU Integration process, http: //www. bacid.eu /images/ 0/02/ Position_Paper_on_the_Western_Balkans_and_local_governments_in_the_EU_integration _%282%29.pdf pp2,8.04.2014

cases can take up to 12 months[85]. On the other hand, NALAS annual Fiscal Decentralization Indicators Report2 shows that SEE local governments' revenues are far below EU average, competences are decentralized without the adequate resources, local governments are dependent on government transfers which results with low investment capacity. Pre-financing thus represents, especially for smaller municipalities a serious bottleneck and obstacle to participate in EU programs. In this regard, support for local governments to access available EU funds and ensure pre-financing of municipal projects through the establishment of a needs-oriented financial instrument would support local governments in preparation and implementation of EU funded projects[86]. A Bridge Funding mechanism could provide for: i) covering temporary shortage of funds in the process of project implementation and ii) financing of ineligible costs, which are important in order to ensure the sustainability and integrity of a project[87]. A very successful Bridge Funding instrument exists in Bulgaria denominated Fund for Local Authorities and Governments, known under its abbreviation FLAG[88]. In order to enhance possibilities of municipalities with insufficient financial resources to participate in EU programs and access EU funding, NALAS recommends the set-up of a Bridge Funding Facility for Local Governments in the region[89]. EU aid facilities in humanitarian and natural disaster situations to support local governments. In 2015, the EU redirected its attention again to the Western Balkans as a result of

---

[85] Western Balkans in the loop, Local Governments and their Associations as key stakeholders in the EU Integration process, http: //www. bacid.eu /images/ 0/02/ Position_Paper_on_the_Western_Balkans_and_local_governments_in_the_EU_integration _%282%29.pdf pp2,8.04.2014

[86] Western Balkans in the loop, Local Governments and their Associations as key stakeholders in the EU Integration process, http: //www. bacid.eu /images/ 0/02/ Position_Paper_on_the_Western_Balkans_and_local_governments_in_the_EU_integration _%282%29.pdf pp2,6.04.2014

[87] Western Balkans in the loop, Local Governments and their Associations as key stakeholders in the EU Integration process, http: //www. bacid.eu /images/ 0/02/ Position_Paper_on_the_Western_Balkans_and_local_governments_in_the_EU_integration _%282%29.pdf pp4, 8.05.2014

[88] Western Balkans in the loop, Local Governments and their Associations as key stakeholders in the EU Integration process, http: //www. bacid.eu /images/ 0/02/ Position_Paper_on_the_Western_Balkans_and_local_governments_in_the_EU_integration _%282%29.pdf pp4,8.05.2014

[89] Western Balkans in the loop, Local Governments and their Associations as key stakeholders in the EU Integration process, http: //www. bacid.eu /images/ 0/02/ Position_Paper_on_the_Western_Balkans_and_local_governments_in_the_EU_integration _%282%29.pdf pp4,8.04.2014

the migration/refugee crisis with the aim to mitigate its repercussions and implications for Union member countries. Municipalities and not central governments along the so-called Balkan route were the frontrunners to face the migration/refugee crisis providing basic services in this unprecedented man-made disaster. Using its resources and shouldering the main burden municipalities depleted its limited resources and compromised their assets and funds and strained their budgets. The unique management of local governments in the migration/refugee crisis should be recognized! Considering the potential risk of renewed migration/refugee movements (returnees and integration) affecting the region, NALAS recommends that adequate support facilities should be provided for local governments in the frame of EU humanitarian and disaster aid facilities. In recent times, social protests in the whole region are piling up, reflecting the political and socio-economic standstill and increasing instability. These events suggest that the Western Balkans candidate countries continue to face deep structural problems. The consequences of the global and European economic crisis, which has hit heavily on the Western Balkans, have certainly been a key factor in recent years and had a negative impact on the EU reform efforts throughout the region that continues to have an effect. But it is the tendency towards autocratic leaderships, the shifting of the balance of power-principle versus a dominant executive branch on the expense of the legislative and judiciary, the infringement on fundamental freedoms, widespread corruption and territorial issues that further threaten stability, peace and democracy as a whole in the region[90]. The crisis reveals an erosion of the covenant between governments, ruling parties and the citizens. This results in a crisis of trust; one no longer relies on the institutions and hardly on the elected politicians. The crisis of trust leads to questioning of hitherto commonly shared values and principles and challenges democracy as a way of life as well as an institutional and structural guideline. And finally, the crisis of the EU model is reflected by increased EU fatigue[91]. RCC's SEE Balkan Barometer 2016 shows that Euro-skepticism is strong in the region as a whole. Findings show that almost 60% of the survey sample have negative or

---

[90] Western Balkans in the loop, Local Governments and their Associations as key stakeholders in the EU Integration process, http: //www. bacid.eu /images/ 0/02/ Position_Paper_on_the_Western_Balkans_and_local_governments_in_the_EU_integration _%282%29.pdf pp5 , 8.05.2014

[91] Western Balkans in the loop, Local Governments and their Associations as key stakeholders in the EU Integration process, http: //www. bacid.eu /images/ 0/02/ Position_Paper_on_the_Western_Balkans_and_local_governments_in_the_EU_integration _%282%29.pdf pp4, 8.05.2014

mixed feelings and are skeptical towards EU membership. NALAS is convinced that a functional bottom-up approach is best suited to contribute to building a sound and sustainable basis for the regional reform process by strengthening local democracy. Bringing the citizen closer to the EU implies going local! What is required is to revert the unsuccessful triple-down effect carried out by the EU for the past 40 years since the Treaty of Rome[92]. This is where LGAs and LGs together can play a crucial role[93]. In fact, it is time to (re)discover the local level as the transmission belt to carry the European ideals of a peacefully united continent into the region and to promote it there bindingly[94]. Laying the foundations of an ever-closer union among the peoples of Europe, to ensure economic and social progress and to improve the citizens' living and working conditions, starts by living and experimenting the EU at local level. We therefore urge under the present circumstances EU institutions to consider LGAs and LG as a crucial stakeholder and strategic partner at local level in the context of EU integration process[95]. We at NALAS advocate as step in the right direction to implement a more inclusive consultation processes at all stages of planning, programming and decision-making on all issues affecting local government by taking into account specific role, tasks and responsibilities of local governments which are different from other local actors (i.e. private and civil sector) and to include the local government dimension in strategic and operational planning for EU enlargement. Well-functioning governing institutions, including those at the local level, are critical for effective and equitable delivery of services, political competition, broad political participation and decision making, and a vibrant and inclusive civil society.1

---

[92] Western Balkans in the loop, Local Governments and their Associations as key stakeholders in the EU Integration process, http: //www. bacid.eu /images/ 0/02/ Position_Paper_on_the_Western_Balkans_and_local_governments_in_the_EU_integration _%282%29.pdf pp6,8.06.2014

[93] Western Balkans in the loop, Local Governments and their Associations as key stakeholders in the EU Integration process, http: //www. bacid.eu /images/ 0/02/ Position_Paper_on_the_Western_Balkans_and_local_governments_in_the_EU_integration _%282%29.pdf pp4,8.06.2014

[94] Western Balkans in the loop, Local Governments and their Associations as key stakeholders in the EU Integration process, http: //www. bacid.eu /images/ 0/02/ Position_Paper_on_the_Western_Balkans_and_local_governments_in_the_EU_integration _%282%29.pdf pp4,8.06.2014

[95] Western Balkans in the loop, Local Governments and their Associations as key stakeholders in the EU Integration process, http: //www. bacid.eu /images/ 0/02/ Position_Paper_on_the_Western_Balkans_and_local_governments_in_the_EU_integration _%282%29.pdf pp6,8.062014

Decentralization involves the devolution of authority over administration, budgets and financial decisions, the allocation of resources, and the provision of services in a manner that is responsive to local communities and largely independent of higher levels of government. Viewing democratic decentralization as part of their neo-liberal strategy, international financial institutions and international organizations (IOs) have championed it in developing countries.3 Donor governments, such as the US, assert that when democratic local governance is combined with decentralization, 'local governments – and the communities they govern—gain the authority, resources, and skills to make responsive choices and to act on them effectively and accountably'.4 In divided post-conflict societies like those in Western Balkans of focus here--Croatia, Bosnia-Herzegovina, Macedonia, and Kosovo--programs to improve the quality of local governance are also expected to provide a context in which social and ethnic conflicts can be constructively addressed out of the harshly politicized light of the national government[96]. Indeed, Socialist Yugoslavia implemented decentralization, albeit within a one-party system because it viewed it as a key mechanism for accommodating ethnicity[97]. Municipalities were considered centers of innovative social self-government reforms, which attracted the attention of Western scholars and practitioners despite the limited power actually devolved. Violence during the 1990s and early 2000s, however, significantly debilitated local governance capacity[98]. Nationalizing elites seeking to strengthen their new states in the face of external and internal threats advocated centralization, which further weakened local governance. During both the socialist and post-conflict period, municipalities possess a civil service, a mayor, and a legislature, and engage in public works projects, basic health care, primary education, local development, and other social welfare programs.8 Though almost none of the municipalities in the post-conflict Western Balkans are ethnically homogeneous, many of them are dominated by one of the country's primary ethnic groups.9 This is particularly the case after the violence of the 1990s, when significant numbers of peoples belonging to ethnic groups who were in the minority in a municipality were forced, or decided to, flee. But they have pressured domestic officials to alter municipal boundaries. International officials pressed Macedonian politicians to redraw municipal

[96] Paula M. Pickering, Assessing International Aid for Local Governance in the Western Balkans
[97] Paula M. Pickering, Assessing International Aid for Local Governance in the Western Balkans pp2
[98] Paula M. Pickering, Assessing International Aid for Local Governance in the Western Balkans pp2,2015

boundaries, including in some cases to increase the proportion of Albanians.10 In Bosnia-Herzegovina (hereafter Bosnia), international officials imposed boundary changes they considered necessary to reunite some municipalities ethnically divided during the war[99]. In the remainder of the paper, I outline the hypothesis derived from post-conflict literature on the impact of internationally supported local governance reforms. I then explore donor and Western Balkan citizens' assessments of local governance reforms[100]. The local governance programs of international donors are outlined and assessed through surveys, interviews, and assessments[101]. Finally, I describe domestic actors' suggestions for improving reforms and discuss the conclusions of field-based research[102]. Expectations from Post-Conflict Literature Comparative analysis of political decentralization reforms suggests that the road leading to an envisioned virtuous outcome of good local governance is littered with potholes, including increased possibilities for political capture. Divided, post-war societies with significant international intervention into domestic politics, such as those in the Western Balkans, present complicated environments for reform. This research was guided by the hypothesis that the greater the degree of international authority in domestic decision-making, the more significant.

the obstacles to developing authoritative domestic institutions for self-sustaining good local governance. This proposition, which builds on critical scholarship on international intervention, asserts that as international authority in domestic policy making increases, arrangements become more complex – the number of foreign decision makers in domestic politics increases and the diversity in basic values, interests, and networks of accountability also increase. The logic argues that this complicates the development of clear and effective domestic mechanisms for decision making and accountability. The hypothesis contends that the heaviest forms of international civilian intervention foster dependency, rather than help build domestic capacity.14 This logic implies that less intrusive international intervention would help better develop political institutions that are more effective and more highly valued by domestic elites and citizens. Knaus and Cox

[99] Paula M. Pickering, Assessing International Aid for Local Governance in the Western Balkans pp3,2015
[100] Paula M. Pickering, Assessing International Aid for Local Governance in the Western Balkans pp3, 2015
[101] Paula M. Pickering, Assessing International Aid for Local Governance in the Western Balkans pp3, 2015
[102] Paula M. Pickering, Assessing International Aid for Local Governance in the Western Balkans pp3,2015

argue for a middle ground approach exercised by the EU. They assert that of the three existing state-building models--the authoritarian, where internationals are vested with executive authority; the traditional, development; and the EU-member state--only the latter's voluntary process that promises the prize of EU membership has been successful. This is because the EU requires aspiring member states to reform their governments to meet democratic standards. Such requirements, EU aid for reforming institutions, and the desire of Western Balkan states to join the EU club supposedly work together to produce an administrative revolution that deepens democracy. Even the lightest international intervention— traditional development assistance for building capacity--confronts obstacles to reform. Multilateral organizations and individual governments' aid agencies often hire intermediaries – international and sometimes local nongovernmental organizations (NGOs)—to implement their aid projects. This generates principal agent relationships that can hinder positive impacts on recipient communities. This 'long aid chain' creates multiple accountability mechanisms and requires cooperation among actors with diverse interests. As McMahon argues in the case of international aid for Bosnian civil society, agents and principals behave in self-interested ways that can 'easily slight the needs of Bosnian society in favour of their own organizations' viability.' International authority in the region's local governance has been the strongest in Kosovo and Bosnia and the weakest in Croatia and Macedonia[103]. The UN Mission in Kosovo initially exercised executive authority which transitioned later into the power to overrule domestic officials up until Kosovo's declaration of independence in winter 2008.21 In Bosnia, the UN High Representative is empowered to impose laws and remove domestic officials at all of Bosnia's multiple levels of governance[104]. In contrast, international officials who co-signed Macedonia's peace agreement in 2001 obligated Macedonia to adopt a revised Law on local self-government that reinforces European standards, but can only assist Macedonian officials in implementing it[105]. In local governance in Croatia, the international role has been largely limited to OSCE and EU monitoring, after the exception of a brief period in a slice of disputed territory in the mid-1990s. All of the countries of focus are also subject to the pull of the EU

---

[103] Paula M. Pickering, Assessing International Aid for Local Governance in the Western Balkans pp5,2015
[104] Paula M. Pickering, Assessing International Aid for Local Governance in the Western Balkans pp5,2015
[105] Paula M. Pickering, Assessing International Aid for Local Governance in the Western Balkans pp5,2015

accession process and development aid. The EC has made additional demands about local governance on Macedonia by making the implementation of decentralization contained in the peace agreement a prerequisite for EU membership. For reformers, the nature of decentralization as a policy issue--on the softer side of security—appears to open greater possibilities for progress though its divisibility into the 'win ' solutions of pork barrel policy making than harder security issues like policing[106]. Decentralization does not fundamentally threaten essential mechanisms of power used by national and regional-level politicians. As a result, the stakes over local governance reform are lower than over reform at the national level of governance. USAID supports local governance. reforms partly out of frustration with efforts to reform central government institutions. The very idea of decentralization invites different degrees of shared ownership (locally, regionally, and nationally) on a variety of components, such as local development and service provision.28 Nonetheless, local governance reforms affect the distribution of political power and thus generate some contention. The politics of decentralization compel international officials to decide whether and how to marginalize or win over powerful domestic actors[107].This is particularly important in Croatia and Bosnia, where officials in powerful intermediate levels of government--counties (županja) in Croatia and entities and cantons in Bosnia-- oppose further devolving power to municipalities[108]. But when policy is viewed in other than zero-sum terms, international officials may use framing to provide a framework to meet multiple interests and build local governing capacity[109]. Nationalist parties, who often control national politics, view favorably their prospects in ethnically-dominated municipalities, making them supportive of decentralization in these circumstances. International officials have tried to bring on board ethnic majority elites, who were initially reluctant to accept internationally backed decentralization they viewed as catering to minority demands for more autonomy, by dangling attractive political prizes. These include Western guarantees for territorial integrity of Bosnia, integration into EU and NATO for Macedonia, and independent statehood for Kosovo. Because of the

---

[106] Paula M. Pickering, Assessing International Aid for Local Governance in the Western Balkans pp5,2015

[107] Paula M. Pickering, Assessing International Aid for Local Governance in the Western Balkans pp7

[108] Paula M. Pickering, Assessing International Aid for Local Governance in the Western Balkans pp7

[109] Paula M. Pickering, Assessing International Aid for Local Governance in the Western Balkans pp5

varying degrees of local ownership and issue-area logic, we expect small, but more significant, progress in local governance reforms in Croatia and Macedonia than in Bosnia or Kosovo[110].

Chapter Seven

1. Relationships between Central and Local Authorities in Kosovo

The European Charter on Local Self-Government (the Charter) was adopted in the form of a convention by the Committee of Ministers of the Council of Europe. It was opened to signature as a convention by the member states of the Council of Europe on 15 October 1985.2 The Charter represents the most important international document delineating the principle of local self-government. It has had considerable influence on the laws of most Council of Europe member states regulating local self-government. The Charter determines that the principle of local self-government shall be recognized in domestic legislation and where practicable in the constitution.3 The concept of local self-government, as envisaged in Article 3 paragraph 1 of the Charter, includes the right and the ability of local authorities, within the limits of the law, to regulate and manage a substantial share of public affairs under their own responsibility and in the interest of the local population. UNMIK Regulation 2007/30 amending UNMIK Regulation 2000/45 on Self-Government of Municipalities in Kosovo in its preamble refers explicitly to the Charter and makes particular reference to its Article 3. In addition to this, the scope of local self-government has been foreseen in Article 4 of the Charter, paragraph 3 of which requires that "[p]ublic responsibilities shall generally be exercised, in preference, by those authorities which are closest to the citizen[111]. Allocation of responsibility to another authority should weigh up the extent and nature of the task and requirements of efficiency and economy." This principle is otherwise known as the principle of subsidiarity. According to the Charter's explanatory report, which is an official source, Article 4 paragraph 3 articulates the general principle that the exercise of public responsibilities should be decentralized. The Charter, apart from making reference to "own" competencies under Article 3, also makes reference to "delegated" competencies in Article 4 paragraph 5. It refrains from defining precisely what affairs local authorities should be entitled to regulate and manage.

---

[110] Paula M. Pickering, Assessing International Aid for Local Governance in the Western Balkans pp7

[111] Relationships between Central and Local Authorities in Kosovo Legal, Administrative and Fiscal Aspects February 2008, -7

This is resulting from the fact that the traditions of the member states of the Charter differ greatly and may vary between countries and over time. However, the intention of the Charter is that local governments should have a broad range of responsibilities which are capable of being carried out at local level.4 In view of that, the Charter in Article 4 defines the scope of local self-government in abstract terms and not with reference to specific areas of competence. In addition it provides that the local authorities, where powers are delegated to them by a central or regional authority, shall be allowed discretion in adapting their exercise to local conditions. Taking into consideration the importance of the principle of subsidiarity, as mentioned in Article 4.3 of the Charter, the Committee of Ministers of the Council of Europe has adopted Recommendation No. R(95) 19 on the implementation of the principle of subsidiarity.5 It recommends to the governments of the member states inter alia to "specify in the relevant legislation a core set of powers pertaining to each level of local and regional authorities in addition to any assumption of general competence; [...] to set up procedures or mechanisms, of a legal or political nature, where these do not already exist, to promote the implementation of the principle of subsidiarity and to deal with any possible associated dispute; to apply all these provisions not only to relations between central government and local authorities, Regarding central level oversight over municipal activities, the Charter foresees in Article 8 such administrative supervision that is provided for by a constitution or statute and exercised in proportion to the interest, which it intends to protect. It should normally be limited to the questions of legality of municipal action and not its expediency[112]. However, an exception is made with regard to delegated competences, where the authority delegating may wish to exercise some supervision over the way in which the task is carried out. With regard to judicial oversight, the Charter in Article 11 calls for the municipalities' right of recourse to a judicial remedy to secure the principle of local self-government[113]. Therefore, Kosovo authorities should take into consideration the principles of the Charter in a future Law on Local Self-Government, which should further define municipal competencies[114]. Within this process, municipalities should be consulted in an

---

[112] Relationships between Central and Local Authorities in Kosovo Legal, Administrative and Fiscal Aspects February, pp8 2008

[113] Relationships between Central and Local Authorities in Kosovo Legal, Administrative and Fiscal Aspects February, pp8 2008

[114] Relationships between Central and Local Authorities in Kosovo Legal, Administrative and Fiscal Aspects , pp8 February, pp8 2008

appropriate way due to the importance of the particular matters that are of concern to them directly. Clear distinctions of competencies at the municipal level would support the exercise of public functions at the municipal level as well as the identification of legal relationships with central level authorities. A future Law on Local Self-Government, which is in compliance with the Charter's principles, would be a step forward for Kosovo on its way towards harmonization of laws with European democratic standards[115]. Competencies of municipalities – future plans Changes in the structure of municipal competencies are likely to happen in the near future. This will probably take the form of a new draft Law on Local Self-Government, which is currently being prepared by the Government, based on the principles contained in the Provisional Institutions of Self-Government's Action Plan for the Implementation of Decentralization (Action Plan). Regardless of whether the Action Plan will be implemented in the current form, it will likely continue to serve as the primary model for the Government's decentralization strategy in Kosovo[116]. The Action Plan foresees as the first step of decentralization a legislative reform. The legislative reform shall include: adoption of three new basic laws (Law on Local Self-Government, Law on Municipal Boundaries and Law on General and Local Election); revision and amendment of the existing legislation having impact on municipal competencies; and adoption of new laws necessary for the local government system[117]. It indicates that local self-government shall be based upon the principles of the European Charter on Local Self-Government, in particular the principle of subsidiarity, and protect and promote internationally recognized human rights standards, having particular regard for the needs of the non-majority communities and their members. According to the Action Plan, the future Law on Local Self-Government shall reinforce the powers and organization of municipalities. The municipal competencies, to be provided for in the future Law on Local Self-Government, are likely to be referred to as municipal own competencies, enhanced own competencies and delegated competencies, in line with the Charter. The own competencies are the core competencies of municipalities, within the scope of which they are entitled to freely regulate and

---

[115] Relationships between Central and Local Authorities in Kosovo Legal, Administrative and Fiscal Aspects February , pp82008
[116] Relationships between Central and Local Authorities in Kosovo Legal, Administrative and Fiscal Aspects February, pp 11 2008
[117] Relationships between Central and Local Authorities in Kosovo Legal, Administrative and Fiscal Aspects February, pp11 2008

manage municipal affairs[118]. Enhanced own competencies are those competencies deriving from an asymmetric decentralization process with the aim of better accommodating the interests of those communities which are not in the majority in the territory of Kosovo[119]. In other words, enhanced own competencies have not been envisaged for all municipalities, but only for municipalities inhabited mostly by the Kosovo Serb community, whereas in the other municipalities these competencies will continue to be exercised by the central level institutions. Delegated competencies are central level competencies that in order to offer better services for inhabitants are exercised by municipalities.

Own competencies Municipalities are likely to have full and exclusive powers in certain areas, while respecting the applicable legislation of Kosovo. The list of competencies currently include: local economic development; urban and rural planning; land use and development; implementation of building regulations and building control standards; local environmental protection; provision and maintenance of public services and utilities; and local emergency response[120]. Such competencies are likely to be provided for in the future Law on Local Self-Government and will be similar for all municipalities across Kosovo[121]. The municipal activities within the areas of own competencies may be subject to administrative review by the central authority. However, such administrative review should be limited to only ensuring whether such activities are in compliance with future constitutional arrangements and the applicable law. Enhanced own competencies Enhanced own competencies are planned to be for certain municipalities where the Kosovo Serb community is in the majority. These enhanced competencies are foreseen in order to address political concerns and better accommodate the needs of the Kosovo Serb community. Examples include: higher education, including registration and licensing of educational institutions; secondary health care, including registration and licensing of health care institutions, recruitment, payment of salaries and training of health care personnel; and cultural affairs, including protection and promotion of Serbian and

---

[118] Relationships between Central and Local Authorities in Kosovo Legal, Administrative and Fiscal Aspects February, pp 11 2008

[119] Relationships between Central and Local Authorities in Kosovo Legal, Administrative and Fiscal Aspects February, pp11 2008

[120] Relationships between Central and Local Authorities in Kosovo Legal, Administrative and Fiscal Aspects, pp11 February 2008

[121] Relationships between Central and Local Authorities in Kosovo Legal, Administrative and Fiscal Aspects, pp12 February 2008

other religious and cultural heritage within the municipal territory, as well as support for local religious communities and enhanced participatory rights in the appointment of Police Station Commanders. By enhancing such competencies[122], the Provisional Institutions of Self-Government would in effect be legitimising parallel structures linked to Belgrade. Such a strategy would allow for integration of existing Serbian parallel structures into the public sector providing services to all the people in Kosovo. Delegated competencies In the future structure, central authorities should continue to be able to delegate competencies to municipalities[123]. There are areas where central uniformity is necessary, such as cadastral records, civil registries, voter registration, business registration and licensing, distribution of social assistance payments (excluding pensions), and forestry protection. Other appropriate competencies can be delegated in accordance with the law[124]. The OSCE advises the legislature to strive for more concise definitions of municipal competencies. Confusion in the exercise of competences should be avoided. The legislature should make an effort to better define municipal competencies in a future Law on Local Self-Government.

Executive oversight Municipalities as basic territorial units, exercise their powers within their areas of responsibilities in order to achieve certain goals and to provide services for the residents as well as to restrict their rights under conditions and procedure determined by the respective laws. In addition to applying the law, municipalities may also legislate within their area of competencies (own and delegated[125]. They can issue municipal regulations to address a multitude of social relations, and municipal decisions to address individual issues. However, both forms of acts require a legal basis in the applicable law, since they are regulating rights and responsibilities of the people in Kosovo . The Charter in its Article 8 takes into account the relationship and points to the principle of legality, differentiates between own and delegated competences and finally stresses the importance of the principle of proportionality. In this part we will examine the current legal framework in view of the extent to which it allows for central level

---

[122] Relationships between Central and Local Authorities in Kosovo Legal, Administrative and Fiscal Aspects, pp12 February 2008
[123] Relationships between Central and Local Authorities in Kosovo Legal, Administrative and Fiscal Aspects, pp12 February 2008
[124] Relationships between Central and Local Authorities in Kosovo Legal, Administrative and Fiscal Aspects, pp12, February 2008
[125] Relationships between Central and Local Authorities in Kosovo Legal, Administrative and Fiscal Aspects, pp13, February 2008

oversight. The second type of oversight includes the right of central authorities to supervise (top down) the activities of municipalities in their areas of competence. Top down central level supervision consists of observation of the municipal activities and directions for their execution. Such supervision still exists, and is likely to be better articulated once there is a new comprehensive law on local self-government. Both types of executive oversight – an appeal against administrative decisions and supervision. The European Charter on Local Self-Government The concept of the local self-government, as reflected in the Charter, denotes the right of local authorities to regulate and manage a substantial share of public affairs under their own responsibility and in interest of the local population (Article 3). The local authorities shall exercise their initiatives up to the extent and nature of the task and requirements of efficiency and economy, i.e., in accordance with the subsidiarity principle and their powers shall not be undermined by another regional or central authority (Article 4). Local authorities shall be entitled to adequate financial resources of their own, of which they may dispose freely within the framework of their powers[126]. The protection of financially weaker local authorities calls for the institution of financial equalization, which should be designed to correct the effects of the unequal distribution of potential sources of finance and of the financial burden they must support. As far as possible the grants to local authorities shall not be earmarked (Article 9). These articles of the Charter form the framework against which the process of fiscal decentralization in Kosovo will be analyzed in this section. Expenditure responsibilities The first pillar of decentralization is the expenditure responsibilities assigned to the municipalities. In the process of fiscal decentralization, municipalities are granted decision-making authority over some government functions and are assigned responsibility to finance the expenditures for managing these functions. The key principle in determining which level of government (central or local) should be responsible to finance the expenditures of the respective function, is the principle of subsidiarity. The subsidiarity principle is used to ensure that public responsibilities are exercised by those authorities which are closest to the citizens (Article 4 of the Charter). Government services should thus be provided at the lowest level of government that is capable of efficiently providing that service[127]. This implies that, "unless the size of the nature of a task is such that it requires to be treated within a larger

[126] Relationships between Central and Local Authorities in Kosovo Legal, Administrative and Fiscal Aspects, pp26 February 2008
[127] Relationships between Central and Local Authorities in Kosovo Legal, Administrative and Fiscal Aspects, pp28 February 2008

territorial area or there are overriding considerations of efficiency or economy, it should generally be entrusted to the most local level of government. Structure and type of transfers a) Purpose of municipal grants The general operating grant is made available to fund all aspects of municipal operations. That means the municipality has full discretionary power to determine on what activities the budget will be spent. Some parts of the general operating grants however are earmarked: the property tax incentive, an amount for education and an amount for health. The property tax incentive program constitutes a part of the earmarked grant. The property tax incentive program funds are available to municipalities only when they achieve the property tax collection target set for a certain year. The municipality, following its internal budget process, identifies capital or investment projects which will be financed from the property tax incentive funds. Such projects are prepared and approved according to public investment program procedures. Other parts of the general operating grant are earmarked for education and health purposes respectively. The education and health grants are structured such that the municipality determines to which education or health units (such as a school or a health house) the grant will be distributed and the amount to be available in the budget for each unit. To the extent that the health and education grants are not sufficient to 34 meet the needs in these areas, the general grant and/or municipal own source revenues should also be directed towards meeting these social needs. b) Distribution of the grants The general operating grant is distributed in two allotments: the first part is a fixed amount distributed to all municipalities equally. The second part is divided between municipalities based on their percentage share in the 2001 official population estimates.98 The amount earmarked for the property tax incentive is withheld from the total general grants amount and appropriated at the beginning of the fiscal year to a municipality subject to its achieving the annual target set for property tax collection. The education grant uses a formula developed by the World Bank which differentiates between majority and minority populations to award a percentage of the funds available. The formula utilized is as follows: for wages and salaries, the number of minority and majority pupils in a municipality is divided by the pupil/teacher ratio for the respective community; for administrative staff the normative number of administrative staff should be used (even though there are no clear and consistent numbers available); for goods and services a fixed amount per school is added to a fixed amount per student differentiated by majority and minority students; for capital outlays 5 euros per student is calculated. The health grant is distributed solely on the percentage of population in the municipality based on the official 2001 population estimates. c) Fair share financing In order to provide adequate protection for communities which are not in the majority in the territory of a municipality, a specific proportion of municipal expenditures should be allocated to those communities in each municipality according to the system of fair share financing. This proportion has been determined by UNMIK regulations on the approval of the Kosovo consolidated budget. According to fair share financing regulations, each municipality should allocate to non-majority communities from their own source revenues, general, education and health grant received from the Kosovo General Budget at least the proportion per municipality in accordance with a schedule indicated in the regulation. The fair share financing should ensure that the needs and legitimate interests of villages, settlements and urban quarters populated by non-majority communities are adequately provided for. The proportions per municipality may be revised periodically to reflect the effects of movements by internally displaced persons or returnees[128]. The proportions can be revised periodically in co-ordination with the ministries of health, education, finance and economy, and the municipal assembly. If municipalities do not meet the set of proportions or do not comply, then sanctions can be imposed. The OSCE considers fair share financing a most important instrument to promote the integration of non-majority communities into Kosovo society. However, in order to assure continued and sufficient support to the principle of fair share financing it is important that the formulas are up to date and accurate. To our knowledge the proportions for fair share financing have not been revised frequently and the method. of revisions is not known. Fair share financing requires solid statistics and regular consultation with municipalities. Even though it is stated that the proportions per municipality for allocating to non-majority communities of the municipality, may be periodically revised in co-ordination with the Ministry of Health, the Ministry of Education, the Ministry of Finance and Economy, the Ministry of Local Government Administration and the municipal assemblies concerned, to our knowledge such a revision has not been initiated. The OSCE recommends updating the formulas for fair share financing in good co-operation with the municipalities of Kosovo. 3. Issues on fiscal equalization Fiscal equalization policy commonly takes two forms: vertical equalization and horizontal equalization. Vertical equalization means that each level of government should have separate and independent revenue sources

---

[128] Relationships between Central and Local Authorities in Kosovo Legal, Administrative and Fiscal Aspects, pp11 February 2008

sufficient to finance the expenditures assigned to that level. In Kosovo the fiscal autonomy of municipalities is rather limited as a result of the fact that in 1999 the interim administration started with a very central system and then continuously has been transferring powers also to the local level. Further transfer of competencies to the local level could be assessed, but would need to be weighed against the level of capacity to plan and manage at the local level. Horizontal equalization implies that there should be a system of transfers that would reduce or eliminate the differences in service provision by tying the transfers to each jurisdiction, to relative tax capacity and to the relative need for and cost of providing public services. Thus, the system needs to take into account that there are differences between municipalities. Also the Charter states that the protection of financially weaker local authorities calls for the institution of financial equalization, which shall be designed to correct the effects of the unequal distribution of potential sources of finance and of the financial burden they must support[129]. The equalization system in Kosovo is implicitly defined in the general grant, out of which a fraction is divided between municipalities based on their percentage share in the 2001 official population estimates. In this regard the population figures are likely to support equalization, since they are not reflecting the migration to the bigger cities in the last years. In general, the financial equalization policies contribute to a certain equal opportunity between local authorities[130]. Their purpose is to moderate the vertical imbalances, to diminish the tax competition, to limit the risks of uncertainties and also to maintain the social cohesion. For the future it needs to be pointed out that systems that are a result of policy decisions taken in the area of fiscal equalization should, however, be explicitly defined in the future Law on Municipal Finances with clearly stated formulas.

Some important matter in future:

Local Self-Government: The future Law on Local Self-Government should be guided by the principles of the European Charter on Local Self-Government[131]. f

---

[129] Relationships between Central and Local Authorities in Kosovo Legal, Administrative and Fiscal Aspects, pp39 February 2008
[130] Relationships between Central and Local Authorities in Kosovo Legal, Administrative and Fiscal Aspects, pp 39 February 2008
[131] Relationships between Central and Local Authorities in Kosovo Legal, Administrative and Fiscal Aspects, pp 39 February 2008

87

The own and delegated competencies should be clearly defined in the new legislation. ƒ Executive oversight over municipal activities needs to be regulated clearly, by taking into account the difference between own and delegated competences. ƒ The legislature should draw a distinction as to when a municipal decision becomes directly subject to judicial review, and when they are subject to administrative review by the central executive bodies. ƒ The legislature should ensure a municipal right of recourse to a judicial remedy in case of a dispute over competencies[132]. ƒ The Ministry of Local Government Administration should repeal Administrative Instruction 2005/7 and address the issue of oversight over municipal activities in the future Law on Local Self-Government, that is currently being drafted. Fiscal Decentralization: ƒ The local government reform process should take into account that finance needs to follow function. Municipal competencies need to be clearly defined in primary legislation as well as respective funds allocated. ƒ The allocation of competences to the local level should be accompanied with a reduction of the dependency ratio, taking into account that an increased amount of own source revenues can facilitate autonomous fiscal and own spending policies at the local level. A future Law on Local Finance needs to introduce a new grant scheme and a further developed role of the Grants Commission. Accurate statistics must be ensured, while the analytical capabilities of officials must be improved at both the central and local level. ƒ A future Law on Local Finance should introduce an explicit horizontal equalization scheme with clearly stated formulae. Prior to this, the fiscal needs and the fiscal capacity of the municipalities should be estimated[133]. A future Law on Local Finance should regulate situations of financial instability and insolvency as well as preconditions and limits for borrowing[134]. A sensitive instrument such as fair share financing requires updating and consultation with municipalities. Central/Local: ƒ In general, the consultation Central/Local: ƒ In general, the consultation and partnership between the local and central government should rest on equality. In that regard, the capacity of the Association of Kosovo Municipalities should be strengthened. ƒ Mechanisms to co-ordinate the relationship between the central and the local level should be strengthened. Here the Association of Kosovo Municipalities could

---

[133] Relationships between Central and Local Authorities in Kosovo Legal, Administrative and Fiscal Aspects, pp 39 February 2008
[134] Relationships between Central and Local Authorities in Kosovo Legal, Administrative and Fiscal Aspects, pp 39 February 2008

play a vital role[135]. ʃ Civil society (the public and NGOs) needs to be encouraged to participate in the municipal budget processes. ʃ Studies of awareness to pay local taxes should be conducted. ʃ Capacity building in the area of financial management is needed, especially at the local level. ʃ A proper monitoring and evaluation system for decentralization should be established at the central government level in close co-operation with the local level. Such monitoring must assess at least the legal framework, its implementation and application at the local level, as well as the need for training and capacity building[136].

Local Governance in Slovenia

1. Local self-government understands the municipal system

The municipal system in which municipalities have been called a socio-political unit had been operating there long since the new local self-government system had replaced the previous system and created new municipalities in size, number of inhabitants, organization, areas of activity. Older former communes were hardly able to compare with the European ones; they were great for being a classically organized municipality and small in terms of cross-regional engagements in Slovenia in terms of efficiency and flexibility of operation of municipalities[137]. The former municipalities have exercised most of their duties on behalf of the state. Research has shown that there was an extraordinarily large increase in duties since 1974 where about 80% of state activities were conducted by municipalities, in accordance with the constitution the municipalities were competent for all public affairs in their territory that were in compliance with general interests except when by law some other situations that the state has encountered)[138]. The municipalities have functioned as an integral part of the state in the first instance. The former communes were both by the number of residents and by the size and the heterogeneity of the tasks that the military exceeded the average of the European municipalities[139]. Even compared to the territorial structure. The former

---

[135] Relationships between Central and Local Authorities in Kosovo Legal, Administrative and Fiscal Aspects, pp 39 February 2008

[136] Relationships between Central and Local Authorities in Kosovo Legal, Administrative and Fiscal Aspects, pp39 February 2008

[137] Relationships between Central and Local Authorities in Kosovo Legal, Administrative and Fiscal Aspects, pp35 February 2008

[138] Relationships between Central and Local Authorities in Kosovo Legal, Administrative and Fiscal Aspects, pp35 February 2008

[139] Relationships between Central and Local Authorities in Kosovo Legal, Administrative and Fiscal Aspects, pp34 February 2008

Slovenian municipalities did not present natural quotation to the local community, 31,740 inhabitants covered the area of 321 km. [140]The organization system has been in the working class system, the delegation system and so on, so that they were later replaced by plurality of property, market economy, multiparty system. The new Slovenian constitution guarantees local self-government to Slovenian citizens according to basic requirements in accordance with international human rights rules and laws and fundamental rights in the allocation of authorizations, the Constitution of Slovenia made it looks like a state in which European standards apply while protecting the rights of local authorities at an administrative level close to the citizen, enabling them to effectively participate in making decisions relevant to their daily lives.[141] In Slovenia, local self-government has been functioning since 1995. Municipalities changed their territories, new legal content with new bodies and so on. Local government reform in Slovenia was in the territorial, financial, material, organizational, administrative and legal content. A lot of changes have been made in Slovenia in recent years, particularly in terms of signing the European Charter in the sphere of territorial competencies of municipalities from the center .The Slovene reform of the self-government concept is not completed and it will continue to be dynamic.[142]

1.2. Reforming elements

The local self-government reform in Slovenia contains five components: functional, territorial, organizational, financial-material and legal component. [143]The functional element implies or re-divides the competencies between the state and municipalities as the basic foundation of local self-government and the implementation of subsidiarity with the process the decentralization that was initiated. The territorial aspect has to do with new arrangements in the creation of new municipalities which replaced the old ones from 62 former communes in 147 new municipalities established in 1994 followed by 45 additional municipalities in 1998 and another established in 2002. [144]Slovenia has 193 municipalities [145]but is

---

[140] Reform in Slovenia
[141] Reform in Slovenia
[142] Reform in Slovenia

[143] Reform in Slovenia
[144] Reform in Slovenia

[145] Reform in Slovenia

not well organized in terms of legal standards. Half of those municipalities that have 5000 inhabitants do not have most of them elementary schools, primary health care, health stations, banks, post offices and facilitating the functioning of municipal bodies. The organizational component has to do with new arrangements in terms of authoritative organization in the municipality which are made up of directly elected troops of the councils and other troops. And the top way of representing the citizens in the decision-making process (civic assembly, referendum and civil initiatives. The financial component -material incorporates the implementation of proportional principles of funds in accordance with the tasks that the local community, solidarity with other municipalities, own sources. The legal component relates to the status of municipalities as a legal entity governed by public law and integration into the complexity of the legal system of the Republic of Slovenia. None of the above mentioned elements Slovenia has met the desired level.

1.3. Financing of Municipalities

Financing or financial resources carry out the functional reality of municipalities with their own resources. Local authorities should have a degree of autonomy within their competencies. Enforcement of these competences implies their own resources. Financial autonomy requires the greatest progress of the transfer of municipal competencies as well as democratic control at the same time and their expenditures. Financial resources must be in accordance with the Constitution and other laws and other municipal regulations. Local public expenditures are approximated as in Cyprus 1.4%, 27.5% Sweden. In Slovenia public spending in 2004 reached 5%. The pragmatism of self-financing and spending can be further co-ordinated with the degree of economic development of the commune and public investment and private investment and donations that may come from the central level.

CONCLUSION

1.Kosovo has accepted ethnic decentralization, which is the only case in the local government developments, through this type of decentralization there are attempts to solve political problems, but political problems have remained where they were, while ethnic decentralization has to do with specific in relation sui - generic with developments in Kosovo. Ethnic Decentralization has a history of itself in Kosovo. First, decentralization was proposed based on the European Charter for Local Administration, then there was an ethnic decentralization happened. In Kosovo there were different views about ethnic decentralization, there were also many political debates, though realistically there is no need for politicization but to provide the most qualitative services for the citizens of all nationalities regardless of what the Constitution of Kosovo says. Kosovo is a special case of decentralization development in the region and Europe and in the world.

2. Kosovo does not have a law on referendums and there is little or no political explanation, why the state cannot have a reference to the needs of the citizens. There are very few debates to issue a law, such a law is quite complex due to of the political situation in Kosovo. Citizens do not have the opportunity to use a democratic problem-solving tool in the municipalities where they live. Referendum as a democratic instrument sees politicized political parties in Kosovo very much. Because of Kosovo's dialogue -Serbia on technical issues has not yet been completed, so there have been many demands of the political nature to be followed by a referendum on many technical and local issues as well as on the level of state affairs to demand expression of the will of the citizens.

3. Kosovo has 38 municipalities with regular functioning, yet the municipality as a basic unit of the state is not understood with great importance in Kosovo. Mostly municipality developments in Kosovo are not very popular with local government acting in local level, if it is compared to the central level of power. In Kosovo it is better to be a mayor municipalities because less media is concerned with municipal problems, Kosovo dominates information coming from the activities of the government, the president, political parties and regional developments and European integrations.

4. The Mayor of the municipality is directly elected by the citizens, and has great authority based on the law on local self-government.

5. In this way of electing the mayor it has often happened that the chairman is elected by a party while most of the local deputies have been from the other party, this has happened to not be effective sometimes with influence in the Municipal Assembly or the work of the assembly is blocked.

6. In Kosovo, local developments also have an impact on the party that leads the Government of Kosovo. This is why the government prevented it from supporting some municipal decisions if was needed assistance from the designated

municipality was requested, such as the purchase of buses from the Municipality of Pristina.

7. The law on Kosovo's capital Pristina has not yet been issued by the Kosovo Assembly; this law should be issued based on the Constitution of Kosovo in Article 13 which has been blocked for a long time by the other party in the Assembly, especially the ruling party of the state. is acceptable and has made Pristina as the Kosovo Croat to enjoy no privilege from its special status in the state of Kosovo.

8. Small municipalities have great difficulties to function based on their own revenues, mainly supported by the national budget, and various international donors.

9. The many established municipalities have not brought up local economic development so far, most of the individual enterprises are working hard and with bank loans, only 35 businesses in Kosovo pay taxes.

10. Municipal services are at a moderate level, and the main problem remains the heating of the city that only the capital of Kosovo Pristina has a public company that includes about 30% of households and businesses that are heating this public enterprise. Almost all municipalities have problems with the heating of houses, mainly for heating use electrical equipment, wood and coal.

11. The road infrastructure is well built, and there are many highways that are being built by the Government of the state,

12. There are many schools which is built in Kosovo in period 2000-2017,now is waiting to build   Pristina Hospital, while the secondary medical service works satisfactorily for the citizens exclude Mitrovica , and as well some small municipalities.

13. Municipal cleaning services still need efficiency, regarding sparkling water almost 90% of Kosovo's citizens have no trouble with drinking water.

14.Local transport is still not good organized.

15. The Association of Serbian Municipalities is an artificial legal entity without a properly regulated status and more dilemma for influences in the level of power in Kosovo. This assembly cannot be established in contravention of the Constitution of Kosovo and the Law on Local Self-Government There are many reactions of the opposition parties about the establishment of this association, some political

parties evaluating this association in contradiction with the legal acts in Kosovo and the violation of the terrorist organization of Kosovo, so far there has been political resistance to the establishment of this very controversial association and sui generis, nowhere in the world, only ethnic communities in Kosovo are attempted to have such a kind of creature.

LITERATURE

Ahtisari Plan for Kosovo

Blerim Burjani, Local Administration, 2007

Constitution of Republic of Kosovo

UNMIK Regulation, 2000/45

UNMIK Regulation, 2000/49

Local Election Law of the Republic of Kosovo

Local Self-Governance Law of Republic of Kosovo

Decentralization: Network of Associations of Local Authorities of South-East Europe

Local Governance Law of Republic of Slovenia

Institute of Kosovo for Political Development

Blerim Burjani was born in Pristina, in capital city of state of Kosovo. Primary and secondary school finish at his birthplace. Law Faculty in the University of Pristina general direction . Magistrates studies at the Law Faculty of the University of Pristina. Until now hold a series of public functions such is Political Adviser to the Minister of Labour and Social Welfare, Political Advisor in the Ministry of Trade and Industry, Representatives of the Government of Kosovo in CEFTA, the former member of the CEC. Blerim has experienc 16 years in high education as a lecturor professor at the Business College, was a professor in the College and University of Pristina ,College Dardania FAMA. In public opinion is known as an expert in development policies and political analyst and executive director of the Kosovo Institute for Development Policy. He has worked for a range of local and international organizations as follows: Council of Europe, KIPA, Human Dynamic in Vienna (Austria), B & S Strategy in Europe, World Bank, UNDP,USAID/RIINVEST, ECMI. He speaks and writes in two international languages: English and Spanish. He lives in Pristina. Books published by author:

The Free Press Society and Democratization (2000)
• Independent Judiciary (2002)
• Independent Judiciary and Human Rights (2004)

• Local administration (2006)

• Human Rights in Kosovo (2008)

• Poor and marginalized groups(2017)

• The State Emergency Situation (2013)

• International Crisis (2010)

• Interpretation of Law (2011)

• Electoral Reform (2014)

• Concept for Kosovo Foreign Policy (2018
    • Employment , Social and Health Protections (2018)

Milton Keynes UK
Ingram Content Group UK Ltd.
UKHW040629170124
436182UK00001B/81